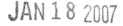
Advance Praise for *Building a Values-Driven Organization: A Whole System Approach to Cultural Transformation*

"We began working with McKinsey to research bank turnarounds out of which was the great story of the turnaround of ANZ bank in Australia under the leadership of John Macfarlane. This in turn led us to Richard Barrett's book *Liberating the Corporate Soul*. The book gave me not only a much clearer insight into culture and values but for the first time provided a way of mapping values and measuring alignment. These concepts and methodologies have been taken to new levels in *Building a Values Driven Organization: A Whole System Approach to Cultural Transformation*. The whole system approach has provided our organization with an extraordinarily powerful practical framework for guiding and driving transformation in every aspect of our organization."
—**Tom Boardman**, Chief Executive, Nedbank Group, South Africa

"Living and leading by values is the foundation for individual and organizational success. It is also the greatest challenge that leaders must confront if they are to truly make a difference. Richard Barrett has further clarified the pathway we can take on that journey; I am grateful for having RBA as a partner as I coach leaders to build values-driven organizations."
—**Tom Brady**, Executive Coach, The XLR8 Team, Inc., Rochester, New York, USA

"At last! A book that focuses on the 'How' rather than the 'What.' The insights in this book represent leading-edge of thinking in whole system change. Richard's passion for making the world a better place through business will move several steps closer as people employ the tools and techniques detailed in this book. Well done, Richard!"
—**David Carter**, Chairman and Founder, Merryck & Co., London, UK

"Richard Barrett at his mind-expanding best. The reptilian part of me frets that our competitors might get this book before it has become part of our DNA."

—**John Elkington**, Chair, Sustainability, London, UK

"Whether you are about to start your cultural transformation or have been working on it for some time, this book will give you a lot of practical and useful tips on how to continue your journey. This book is a must for anyone who wants to understand and manage successful cultural transformation."

—**Tor Eneroth**, Culture Manager, Volvo Information Technology, Gothenberg, Sweden

"Richard Barrett has masterfully integrated the key dimensions of cultural transformation in a very clear, concise, and practical way. The book is a compelling invitation for leaders and change agents to embark on the journey toward self-actualization and organizational greatness for the global common good."

—**Alain Gauthier**, Associate author of *Action Inquiry: The Secret of Timely and Transforming Leadership* and author of the forthcoming book *The Inner Dance of Partnering*

"Richard Barrett lays a vital foundation that helps all business leaders understand not only why change is difficult but how to make it happen. *Building a Values-Driven Organization* goes to the core of what drives change and sustains systems: what motivates and influences us as individuals. This link between strategic goals on the macro level and individual behavior is invaluable for anyone involved in effecting a cultural change. For practitioners in the area of business ethics and compliance, Barrett's analysis is the most innovative to date in helping build a true integrity-based culture by looking at the values and motivations of individual employees and managers that drive ethical behavior."

—**David Gebler**, President, Working Values, Ltd., Sharon, Massachusetts, USA

"If you want your organization to consistently perform at peak levels, you need to become values-driven—a company that is characterized by strong alignment between individual values and corporate values; a company characterized by strong alignment between individual and group sense of mission; a place where the 'walk' matches the 'talk.' And it all starts with you, the leader. Whatever the current state of your organization, Richard Barrett's *Building a Values-Driven Organization* is a must read. The cynics in the audience may see his call for self-actualized leaders creating a values-driven future for business as 'pie in the sky.' However, as someone who has hired Richard as a consultant to work with our business, I can assure you this is a practical, how-to guidebook. You will be amazed at the response from your organization and the resulting manifold benefits for your employees, your customers, and the results of your firm."
—**Grant Kvalheim**, Co-President, Barclays Capital, New York, USA

"Richard Barrett shows us how to make sense of the yearning to create organizations that are more productive and more profitable and also more satisfying places in which to work. This is a first-class, practical, book that any business, government or nonprofit agency can use to good advantage. It should be read by anyone who believes values shape behavior. And it should certainly be read by anyone who does not. Barrett is smart. More importantly, he is wise."
—**Susan A. Lieberman Ph.D.**, Director, Leadership Rice, Rice University, Houston, Texas, USA

"Managing your enterprise and your life through values is the path to follow to achieve self-realization. Richard Barrett gives us an excellent guide to accomplish this cultural transformation."
—**Oscar José Rodríguez López**, President and Managing Director, Venezuela and Andean Pact Countries, Bridgestone Firestone, Valencia, Venezuela

"Richard's new book makes me think of a quote Gandhi made: 'Be the change and you'll be the world.' Indeed, organizational transformation always starts with the personal transformation of the executive team. The deepest connection that bonds people together is shared values. In a very clear and comprehensive way this book explains how one can enhance this bonding, create an atmosphere of wellbeing at work, and improve performance. A must-read for every leader."
—**Adelheid Maekelberg**, Head of Service Training, Coaching and Development, Banksys, Belgium

"As a former leader of an organization that was listed as one of the most values-aligned companies, this book truly represents my experience. Barrett's brilliance is in taking highly complex models and making them understandable for practitioners to follow. For consultants, this book is a comprehensive resource for transforming organizations and is full of leading-edge thinking. This book is a must-read for anyone who wants to create a values-driven organization. More than that, it is a must-read for anyone who wants their organization to have long term success!"
—**Bambi McCullough**, Partner, Chrysalis Partners and former Executive Vice President of Sterling Bank, Houston, Texas, USA (listed on Fortune's 100 Best Companies to Work for 2002, 2003 & 2004)

"When I reflect on what makes an outstanding organization, I keep coming back to the effectiveness of our people, individually and collectively. Our responsibility as leaders therefore is to enhance, harness, and direct the capacity and energy of our people towards virtuous and valuable ends. Long-term success has to have a solid foundation built on principles and values that act as a center of gravity. In business, you get what you target, design, measure, provide incentives for, and are passionate about. This applies equally to principles and values, which need to be nurtured and directed through an effective whole systems approach and values-management framework. This is exactly what Richard Barrett

provides in *Building a Values-Driven Organization*. As an active and experienced user of Richard Barrett's Cultural Transformation Tools, I commend his ideas and frameworks to anyone who is committed to a values-based approach and to long-term sustainable success."
—**John McFarlane**, Chief Executive Officer, ANZ Bank, Melbourne, Australia

"Brilliant! Absolutely brilliant! Barrett has taken the best practices in conscious business transformation and integrated them seamlessly with the wisdom of the ages on levels of consciousness. This book is intellectually stimulating, spiritually awakening, and incredibly practical and hands-on."
—**Judi Neal, Ph.D.**, Executive Director, Association for Spirit at Work; Founder, International Spirit at Work Awards; and President, Neal & Associates

"*Building a Values-Driven Organization* is an extraordinary contribution to the world of business and full of practical and profound ways to help create a better world. It simply gets straight to the heart of what is required for whole systems change in business."
—**Helen-Jane Nelson**, Cecara Consulting, London, UK

"Richard Barrett is the world's leading thinker in creating values-based organizations. This new book is his most wonderful gift yet to practitioners and business leaders alike."
—**Michael Rennie**, Director, McKinsey and Company, New York, USA

"This book succeeds in helping companies to understand their organizational values. It introduces the revolutionary concept and technology of values management. It is widely utilized among merging companies in Japan."
—**Shogo Saito**, Chairman, Business Consultants, Inc., Tokyo, Japan

Building a Values-Driven Organization:
A Whole System Approach to Cultural Transformation

Building a Values-Driven Organization

Organization

A Whole System Approach to Cultural Transformation

Richard Barrett

ELSEVIER

AMSTERDAM · BOSTON · HEIDELBERG · LONDON
NEW YORK · OXFORD · PARIS · SAN DIEGO
SAN FRANCISCO · SINGAPORE · SYDNEY · TOKYO

Butterworth Heinemann is an imprint of Elsevier

Butterworth–Heinemann is an imprint of Elsevier
30 Corporate Drive, Suite 400, Burlington, MA 01803, USA
Linacre House, Jordan Hill, Oxford OX2 8DP, UK

Recognizing the importance of preserving what has been written, Elsevier prints its
books on acid-free paper whenever possible.

Library of Congress Cataloging-in-Publication Data

Barrett, Richard, 1945-
  Building a values-driven organization : a whole system approach to cultural
transformation / by Richard Barrett.
      p.   cm.
  ISBN 0-7506-7974-3
  1. Social responsibility of business.   2. Industrial management—Social aspects.
3. Business ethics.   I. Title.
HD60.B378 2006
658.4'08—dc22

                                                              2005032357
British Library Cataloguing-in-Publication Data
A catalogue record for this book is available from the British Library.

ISBN 10: 0-7506-7974-3
ISBN 13: 978-0-7506-7974-9

For information on all Elsevier Butterworth–Heinemann publications visit our Web site
at www.books.elsevier.com

Printed in the United States of America
06 07 08 09 10   10 9 8 7 6 5 4 3 2 1

Dedication

To those who have dedicated their lives to building a better world through business.

Table of Contents

Preface

This book was a new experience for me. The two books I had written previously, and the one I have in preparation, have consumed years of time in research and preparation. I often tell people that I cannot write a book in less than 3 years. Apart from the research, what takes time is the synthesis of simplicity from complexity, the distillation of wisdom from experience, and simple reflection—just letting the data speak—letting what wants to emerge unfold in its own time. Never rushing this emergence; always nurturing what wants to come forward and bringing it to the light of day in the most meaningful way possible. That is my usual experience. Not this book. Four years into writing what I have labeled my *magnum opus*, a book entitled *Love, Fear and the Destiny of Nations: An Exploration of the Role of Business and Government in the Evolution of Consciousness of Humanity*, I felt this uncompromising urge to start writing *Building a Values-Driven Organization*. Six months later it was done. Finished. No agonizing over structure, no contemplation over content, no time for reflection. It was an infant that was way past due. It needed to emerge. It shouted and screamed at me to let it come into the world.

And so, I offer you this book; a book that summarizes 8 years of experiences; a book that was being written in the background of my mind while my consciousness was focused on my work; a book that wants to be read.

So What's in This Book?

Chapter 1 picks up the storyline of my working life in 2003—5 years after publishing *Liberating the Corporate Soul*. Having spent almost all of this period (1998–2003) focused on mapping the values of organizations and developing and perfecting our cultural transformation programs, I began to experience a need to look around and see what others were doing. It was at this point that I realized there was a wealth of methodologies and technologies available for cultural transformation but they were mostly being used in a stand-alone manner. No one was attempting to integrate them. I felt an urge to explore this possibility. Chapter 1 tells this story—it provides the background to my research and explores the key concepts contained in *Building a Values-Driven Organization*. If you are a person who normally reads the last chapter first, I would suggest *this time* you read the first chapter first—it will give you the whole plot.

Chapter 2 picks up the threads of my second book, *Liberating the Corporate Soul*, by reminding the reader of the seven levels of consciousness model as it applies to individuals and groups. This chapter contains new insights not previously published elsewhere.

Chapter 3 moves from the model to the tools—the cultural transformation tools (CTT). It provides a detailed account of the latest version of the cultural transformation tools and how the cultural transformation tools are used to map the values of organizations.

Chapter 4 provides a specific case study of the use of the CTT. It also describes some of the major insights and learning gleaned over the past 8 years from client engagements.

Chapter 5 describes the process we use for mapping the values of individuals, showing how the results of the CTT individual values assessment can be used for coaching.

Chapter 6 illustrates how the cultural transformation tools are used in mergers and acquisitions to explore the cultural compatibility of two organizations. This leads us to explore the role of the leaders in defining the culture of organization. We have taken this work a step further by identifying five basic types of culture that reflect the impact that the leadership group has on the rest of the organization.

Chapter 7 explores in great detail my most well know quote: Organizational transformation begins with the personal transformation of the leadership group. Organizations don't transform. People do! The main focus of this chapter is on the demonstration of the use of the leadership values assessment (LVA)—one of the cultural transformation tools—as a coaching tool.

Chapter 8 moves from the perspective of the personal transformation of the leadership group to the perspective of cultural transformation of the whole organization. It describes the key components of the integral change model—personal alignment, group cohesion, and structural alignment, and discusses the concept of whole-system change.

Chapter 9 provides a framework for cultural transformation that integrates different models, tools and techniques into a comprehensive whole-system change process. It provides a step-by-step description of the preparation and implementation phases.

Chapter 10 presents the research on decision-making that I have been doing as part of the preparation for my book, *Love, Fear and the Destiny of Nations*. It describes the four vectors of consciousness and the five modes of decision making. It also discusses the relevance of each of these modes of decision making in an organizational environment.

Chapter 11 for me, represents the core of this book: How to use the cultural transformation tools to actively manage the values of an organization. I present a dashboard of key performance indicators for monitoring the culture of an organization and the shifts in values and behaviors of the executive population.

Chapter 12 shows through examples how to use the technique of appreciative inquiry to develop sets of behaviors for each of the organization's espoused values.

Chapter 13 focuses on the topic of resilience: How to build a sustainable, long-lasting organization that can withstand shocks and transform under conditions of prolonged duress. It covers the topics of cultural, operational, and structural resilience, and how to increase the adaptive capacity of an organization.

Chapter 14 provides an example of how business is learning to develop a more integral or holistic approach to organizational evaluation. This chapter describes the work of The Centre for Integral Excellence at Sheffield Hallam University in combining the EFQM excellence model and the cultural transformation tools. A case study involving the University's facilities directorate is presented.

Chapter 15 concludes with a reminder of the importance of values-based decision-making; the need for leadership training programs that build full-spectrum, self-actualized leaders; and the urgent need to create a global cadre of master practitioners of whole-system change to support our business and political leaders in creating a values-driven future for business, society and humanity.

The appendix provides contact and resource information for those who are interested in following up on some of the ideas contained in this book.

Acknowledgments

There are many people that I would like to thank for their encouragement in writing this book. Since I cannot separate my work from my life the list must begin with my wife, Nancy, who is a constant loving support to everything that I do. I would also like to thank those with whom I interact everyday and who have been a sounding board for my ideas— my business partners Joan Shafer, Chris Gomez, Phil Clothier, and Ed Manning. I also thank Nathan Egge, Bonnie Roxby, Liz Hamilton, and Lynn Zullo who support us with their technical expertise and joyfully keep our lives in order. A particular word of thanks goes to Ella Long who helped me edit the final manuscript.

Next, I would like to thank the hundreds of people around the world who are part of the CTT network and who share the same vision. Everyday, they courageously take up the challenge of building a better world through business. Tough work at times, but worth the long hours they put in. This book has been written to help and sustain them on their journey.

Special thanks also go to John Smith who financed the Whole-System Change Summits, and the core team who gave up significant amounts of time to contribute their ideas at the summit meetings: Don Beck, Christopher Cooke, Frank Dixon, Bruce Gibb, Marilyn Hamilton, Ben Levi, Helen-Jane Nelson, Mike Pupius, Tom Rautenberg, Michael Rennie,

Joan Shafer, Sonia Stojvanovic, Sander Tideman, Susan Vance, and Steve Trevino. Numerous others also participated in specific meetings.

I would also like to thank those who contributed to the writing process by helping me understand the details of their fields of expertise: Sallie Lee for appreciative inquiry, Sally Mizerak for balanced scorecard, Don Beck for spiral dynamics, Steve Trevino for resilience, Erik Muten and Kathy Davison for theater, Morel Fourman for performance management, and Mike Pupius for the EFQM excellence model.

Finally, I want to thank those who provided feedback and comments on this book during its preparation: Mary-Jane Bullen, Eric Muten, Joan Shafer, Robert Taylor, and Phil Wilson.

Prologue

One of the many things that impressed me about Richard's last book, *Liberating the Corporate Soul: Building a Visionary Organization*, was the epigraph written by the late Willis Harman, who was co-founder of the World Business Academy. Willis wrote:

> Business has become the most powerful institution on the planet. The dominant institution in any society needs to take responsibility for the whole. But business has not had such a tradition. This is a new role, not well understood or accepted. Built on the concept of capitalism and free enterprise from the beginning was the assumption that the actions of the many units of individual enterprise, responding to market forces and guided by the "invisible hand" of Adam Smith, would somehow add up to desirable outcomes. But in the last decade of the twentieth century, it has become clear that the "invisible hand" is faltering. It depended on a consensus of overarching meanings and values that is no longer present. So business now has to adopt a tradition it has never had throughout the entire history of capitalism: to share responsibility for the whole. Every decision that is made, every action that is taken, must be viewed in light of that responsibility.

I found out later, when I met Richard, that he and Willis were good friends. I am not surprised. Richard and Willis share the same lucid, logical visionary approach to their work.

I have to admit, I was so impressed by Richard's last book I could not put it down. I read it 5 times. I have spent the last 6 years introducing his concepts into my business and into my personal life; and I am not the only one. Chief executive officers (CEOs) in more than 35 countries on all continents are using Richard's cultural transformation tools to build long-lasting, values-driven, sustainable organizations.

I believe we will look back in a few years and recognize *Liberating the Corporate Soul* as a timely classic. It was certainly instrumental in changing my perspective and that of many other business leaders like me. It came across my desk at a time when we were beginning to ask some big questions about business, particularly around the vision, mission, and underlying purpose of business. *Liberating the Corporate Soul* provided many of the answers we were looking for.

Richard's new book, *Building a Values-Driven Organization*, is just as timely. The baby boomer–fueled economic miracle of the last 25 years is coming to a rapid end. The war for talent that McKinsey wrote about almost 10 years ago has finally kicked in with a vengeance. Downsizing and relentless delayering have resulted in the accelerated promotion of young professionals. The CEOs of the business divisions of large multinationals are about 15 years younger than they were 20 years ago.

As I mentor CEOs throughout Europe, North America, and Australia, I am finding an increasing number of them not only questioning our existing business models but reinventing them. And, that is where this *Building a Values-Driven Organization* comes in. As business leaders, we have all known for years what we needed to do to reinvent our businesses. What has been missing is the *how* to do it.

Richard's elegant and simple model for whole-system change gives us the how. This is exactly what CEOs need–tools, methodologies, and a process for managing corporate cultures and corporate values.

If I had a dollar for every book or article that I have read in the last 5 years about how messed up the planet is and how important the role of business is in turning the situation round, I could have retired a long time ago. What many of the leaders I work with have worked out is that in order to transform their organizations they have to start by transforming themselves. Richard's now famous quote from *Liberating the Corporate Soul*, summarizes this precisely:

Organizations don't transform. People do!

As a consequence, over the past few years, personal mastery has become the backbone of my work. Once I have helped a leader establish a sense of personal vision, mission, and purpose, the next logical question they ask is "How do I extend this self-knowledge and awareness to my organization? How do I unleash the potential of my people in a way that is sustainable and that has integrity?" For many this has proved to be a difficult and illusive journey. The solution was to be found inside what leading-edge management consultants have been referring to as "whole-system" or "total culture" change. They were almost right. What was needed was whole-system transformation.

Change to me is when the same thing emerges from a process but has an "er" at the end of the new descriptor. The new culture has become lean"er," fitt"er," fast"er," cheap"er," and so forth. Transformation on the other hand is when a caterpillar becomes a butterfly: When you cannot recognize what is emerging from what existed before. Because of the high levels of entropy built into our current business cultures, change is not enough. What is called for is whole-system transformation.

Now we are clear about what needs doing, *Building a Values-Driven Organization* will help CEOs, human resources directors of businesses, and the thousands of consultants who are working on cultural issues around the world to answer the vital question of "How?"

William Wilberforce (1759–1833), a former British Prime Minister who was instrumental in banning slavery, and coincidentally was born in the same town as Richard, said the future is about the "restoration of business manners" or more simply put in today's vernacular: "[it's about] Doing the right things and doing them the right way." It is about sustainability, service, and liberating the soul of our organizations—making decisions that resonate with the most deeply held values of our employees and our customers.

Willis Harman and Richard Barrett are asking us to think bigger—to think about the role of business in creating a better world for everyone—not just for our children, but our children's children. In truth, their vision is the only outcome possible. We can waste more time satisfying the miserly needs and the greed of our egos or we can choose to create a future that makes us feel good inside—that lifts our souls and at the same time builds a sustainable future for everyone—for business and society.

I believe *Building a Values-Driven Organization* is the answer to the challenge that Willis Harman wrote about more than a decade ago.

Enjoy the journey,
David Carter
Chairman and Founder
Merryck & Co.
david.carter@merryck.com

1

Introduction

Background

My purpose in writing this book is to develop and build on the ideas contained in *Liberating the Corporate Soul: Building a Visionary Organization*[1]
published in 1998. The basic premise of *Liberating the Corporate Soul* was
that the most successful organizations on the planet are vision-guided and
values-driven. The results of mapping the values of more than 500 companies in 35 countries since 1997 support this premise—values-driven
companies are without a doubt, the most successful companies on the
planet. Many other researchers also support this conclusion.[2-4] Therefore,
I will not spend much time on making this case. Rather, I prefer to take
this opportunity to draw on our own[5] experiences and the vast amount

---

[1] Richard Barrett. *Liberating the Corporate Soul: Building a Visionary Organization.* Boston: Butterworth-Heinemann, 1998.

[2] James C. Collins and Jerry I. Porras. *Built to Last: Successful Habits of
Visionary Companies.* New York: HarperBusiness, 1994.

[3] Jim Collins, *Good to Great.* New York: HarperBusiness, 2001.

[4] Lynn Sharp Paine. *Value Shift.* New York: McGraw-Hill, 2003.

[5] Richard Barrett & Associates.

of data we have collected over the past 8 years to describe the key characteristics of values-driven organizations; explain how to build values-driven organizations; and show how the process of values management can be used to support continuous improvements in organizational performance and develop long-term sustainability. In addition, I will detail the improvements we have made to the cultural transformation tools since the publication of *Liberating the Corporate Soul.*

There are many new ideas in this book that have not previously been published and cannot be found in mainstream management or organizational development literature. Examples include, the concepts of cultural resilience[6] and cultural entropy,[7] the five modes of decision making, and the integration of mature and emergent technologies into a comprehensive methodologic framework for whole-system change.

In my opinion, the two most important topics explored in this book are as follows:

(1) A whole-system or "integral" approach to cultural transformation; and

(2) Values management—measuring, monitoring, and responding to causal indicators of performance (values and behaviors) to adjust the culture of an organization so that it is able to sustain high performance and mission assurance.[8]

---

[6] Cultural resilience is defined as the ability of an organization or any human system to withstand shocks and remain sustainable under prolonged conditions of duress.

[7] Cultural entropy is defined as the proportion of energy in an organization or any human system that is consumed by nonproductive activities such as bureaucracy, internal competition, empire building, and so forth.

[8] Mission assurance is defined as the ability of an organization to deliver high quality products or services under all operating conditions. This is important for both corporations and public sector services.

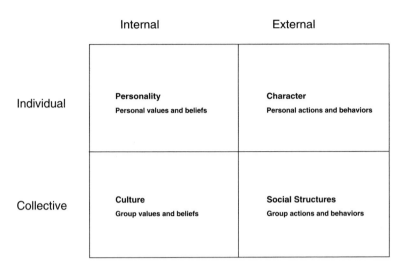

Internal   External

Individual

Personality
Personal values and beliefs

Character
Personal actions and behaviors

Collective

Culture
Group values and beliefs

Social Structures
Group actions and behaviors

Figure 1–1   The four quadrants of human systems

The concept of whole-system change described in this book is based on the work of Ken Wilber.[9] I can best explain what is meant by whole-system change by referring to Figure 1–1, a modified version of Ken Wilber's Four Quadrant Model.

The quadrants represent the four different perspectives one can have on human systems:

- The perspective from the internal of the individual—individual consciousness—personal values and beliefs.
- The perspective from the external of the individual—personal actions and behaviors.
- The perspective from the internal of a collective—group consciousness—cultural values and beliefs.
- The perspective from the external of a collective—group social structures, systems, processes, actions, and behaviors.

[9] Ken Wilber. *A Brief History of Everything.* New York: Shambhala, 1996; p. 71.

To make this model more directly applicable to groups, organizations, and institutions, I have simplified Wilber's four-quadrant model by using personal values and beliefs as a proxy for the internal consciousness of an individual and personal actions and behaviors as a proxy for what is externally observable about an individual. Similarly, I have used group values and beliefs as a proxy for the collective consciousness of the group (culture), and group actions and behaviors as a proxy for what is externally observable about a group (social structures and behaviors).

As individuals change their values and beliefs, their actions and behaviors change. When a critical mass of individuals changes their values and beliefs in the same direction, their collective actions and behaviors also change. For this to happen, there must be a parallel shift in all four quadrants.

Engineering parallel shifts in the four quadrants within a group structure such as an organization or any human system is called "whole-system change." Whole-system change begins with a shift in the personal consciousness of individuals and ends with a shift in the group's actions and behaviors. Organizations don't transform. People do! This means that if we can define a map of the territory we call consciousness; we can make the evolution of consciousness, conscious. We can intentionally engineer a shift from one level of consciousness to the next by managing the values of an organization. This is a major new idea pregnant with possibilities for improving the way we grow and develop our organizations. The purpose of values management is therefore to actively measure and monitor the values and behaviors of an organization so that we can continually adjust the culture to sustain high performance.

Whole-System Change

The idea for developing a whole-system approach to cultural transformation began to occupy my mind early in 2003. I had recognized for some time that there were several different models and tools in the market place for supporting cultural transformation, all of which were successful in their own way. It seemed to me that what was required was an overarching framework that would allow these models and tools to be combined in a more meaningful and beneficial approach.

My thought at that time was "How much more successful would these approaches be if they could be integrated into a broader more comprehensive methodology that encompassed whole-system change?" My business partner, Joan Shafer, and I had already integrated the technology known as *appreciative inquiry*[10] into our framework for implementing cultural transformation, but I knew there was more that could be done.

It was at this point in time that I had a life-changing meeting with John Smith, chief executive officer (CEO) of HearthStone Homes—an Omaha-based home construction company. I had advised John and his company on matters of organizational culture for several years. It was at the end of a transformation weekend program that I was putting on for John and his business partner that John asked me about my future plans. I immediately told him about my idea for developing a whole-system approach to cultural transformation that integrated different technologies.

Without hesitating, he said he would support me in this venture by funding a series of meetings that brought together thought leaders and key organizational practitioners from around the world to discuss the development of a whole-system approach to cultural transformation. The series of meetings known as the "Whole-system Change Summits" began in the fall of 2003. Many of the insights contained in this book

---

[10] David L. Cooperrider, Peter F. Sorensen Jr., Diana Whitney, and Therese F. Yaeger, eds. *Appreciative Inquiry: Rethinking Human Organization Toward a Positive Theory of Change.* Champaign, IL: Stipes Publishing, 2000.

are based on reflections and recommendations emanating from these meetings.

The collective experiences of this group suggest that there are three basic requisites for successful whole-system change. First, the leaders of the group have to drive the process of change. They need to be committed to, and become exemplars of the vision, mission, values, and behaviors—they must "walk the talk." The change must begin with the personal transformation of the leadership group.

Second, the vision, mission and values as well as the supporting behaviors should influence all decision-making. The values and behaviors should be reflected in every aspect of the group's structures, systems and processes. For example, in organizations, the values and behaviors should be reflected in the way employees, managers, and executives are selected, in the content of new-employee orientation programs, in the scope of management and executive development programs, in the way talented individuals are selected and nurtured, in promotion criteria, in leadership development programs, and in performance management, and so forth. Every aspect of "the way things are done around here" need to be in alignment with the vision, mission, values, and behaviors.

Third, for sustainable high performance, the culture must be comprehensively monitored through the measurement of individual and collective "causal" performance indicators (values and behaviors). One of the main reasons why companies do not reach their full potential or fail is because they do not monitor their cultures. There is no early-warning dashboard to indicate a rise in cultural entropy or a decrease in cultural resilience.

In conclusion, for whole-system change to be successful, the values of the organization should be pervasive. They should drive all aspects of decision-making and be reflected in every system and process. They should underpin and be reflected in the individual behaviors of the leaders, managers and staff and the collective behaviors of the organization. They should become part of the organization's cultural DNA.

Implementing Whole-System Change

It is impossible to define a single whole-system approach to cultural transformation because the implementation methodology differs according to the levels of consciousness, worldviews, and motivational drivers of the leaders, the managers, and the employee population. That is why I refer to the process of whole-system change as a framework. The framework or key stages in the process of whole-system change are relatively well established and fixed; the technologies within the framework are changeable and fluid depending on the levels of consciousness, worldviews, and motivational drivers of the leaders, managers, and staff.

Furthermore, the culture change technologies that are appropriate for corporations may be different from those that are appropriate for government agencies or nongovernmental organizations. The methodology and techniques used in a whole-system change process need to reflect what is acceptable and appropriate for the levels of consciousness, worldviews, and motivational drivers of the people involved.

For example, we often find in corporations that the leaders, because of their worldviews and motivational drivers, are unwilling to involve everyone in the organization in defining the vision, mission, and values of the organization. The main reason for this reluctance is that they operate from levels of consciousness that require them to stay firmly in control. They feel responsible and accountable to the shareholders for the success of the organization. They are not at ease with uncertainty and find it difficult to trust others. I am not saying that this need to stay firmly in control is right or wrong; it is simply a factor that must be taken into account by those who are designing and guiding the process of change.

In such situations, approaches and techniques such as *appreciative inquiry*[11] and *open space*,[12] which are designed to give everyone a voice in developing the vision and mission of an organization, may not be appropriate. Other methodologies, such as the *four-whys process*, described in *Liberating the Corporate Soul*, may be more acceptable. What we have learned over the past few years is that the choice of cultural transformation techniques is significantly dependent on the consciousness of the leadership group and executive population.

For the "hard-nosed" businessperson, "soft" approaches that explore the inner world of emotions and the role of ego and the soul in decision-making are off the radar screen. They simply cannot be accommodated in the belief structures that they hold. It is vital therefore, that every element of the whole-system change process be tailored to the level of consciousness and belief structures of the executive and employee population. You have to meet people where they are before you can take them where they want to go.

We have found that the approach to cultural transformation in the private sector needs to be different from the approach used in the public sector, and the approach used in banking needs to be different from the approach used in manufacturing. Similarly, what works in the United States may not work in Europe, and what works in Europe may not work in Asia or South America. Different cultures emphasize different levels of consciousness and operate with different worldviews. I repeat—you have to know where people are, to design a process to take them to where they want to go.

[11] Ibid.

[12] Harrison Owen. *Open Space Technology: A User's Guide.* San Francisco: Berrett-Koehler, 1997.

These are perhaps the three key insights we have uncovered over the past 8 years:

(1) A "cookie-cutter" approach to the design of cultural transformation programs in organizations (or any human system), where one size fits all, does not work. It may work in some situations, but not in others. Generally speaking, proprietary approaches to cultural transformation are not sufficiently flexible to accommodate all situations. They are hit and miss.

(2) Cultural transformation will only work if it is part of a whole-system change process. People will not change how they operate if the underlying structures, processes, and reward systems do not change also.

(3) Cultural transformation will only succeed if the leadership team is committed to this work.

As a consultant or change agent, it is vital that you understand what levels of consciousness and what worldviews different segments of the executive and employee population are operating from if you are going to successfully design and support the leaders of an organization in managing a whole-system transformation process.

2

The Seven Levels of Consciousness Model

There are three models at the heart of the whole-system approach to cultural transformation: the seven levels of consciousness model, the spiral dynamics model, and a modified version of Ken Wilber's Integral (four-quadrant matrix) model. The seven levels of consciousness model is described in my book, *Liberating the Corporate Soul: Building a Visionary Organization.*[1] The spiral dynamics model is described in Beck and Cowan's *Spiral Dynamics: Mastering Leadership and Change.*[2] The integral model is described in Ken Wilber's *A Brief History of Everything.*[3] My modified version of the integral model is described in Chapter 8 and an overview of the spiral dynamics model is included in Chapter 9. What follows in this chapter, and the next, is a detailed description of the seven levels of consciousness model as it applies to individuals, groups, and organizations.

[1] Richard Barrett. *Liberating the Corporate Soul: Building a Visionary Organization.* Boston: Butterworth-Heinemann, 1998; pp. 55–72.

[2] Don Edward Beck and Christopher C. Cowan. *Spiral Dynamics: Mastering Values, Leadership and Change.* Cambridge, MA: Blackwell, 1996.

[3] Ken Wilber. *A Brief History of Everything.* Boston: Shambhala, 1996: pp. 69–83.

The Seven Levels of Personal Consciousness

Seven well-defined stages can be distinguished in the development of personal consciousness. Each stage focuses on a particular existential need that is inherent to the human condition. The seven existential needs are the principle motivating forces in all human affairs. Individuals grow in consciousness by learning to master the satisfaction of these needs. Individuals who learn how to master all seven needs without harming or hurting others operate from full-spectrum consciousness. They have the ability to respond appropriately to all life's challenges. The seven existential needs that constitute the seven stages in the development of personal consciousness are shown in Table 2–1.

Table 2–1   The Seven Stages/Levels of Personal Consciousness

Level	Motivation	Focus
7	Service	Leading a life of self-less service
6	Making a difference	Making a positive difference in the world
5	Internal cohesion	Finding personal meaning in existence
4	Transformation	Finding freedom by letting go of our fears about survival, feeling loved, and being respected by our peers
3	Self-esteem	Feeling a sense of personal self-worth
2	Relationship	Feeling safe, respected, and loved
1	Survival	Satisfying our physical needs

The "lower" or basic needs, levels 1 to 3, focus on our need for physical survival, our need for physical and emotional safety, and our emotional need for self-esteem. The "higher" needs, levels 5 to 7, focus on our "spiritual" needs—the need to find meaning in our lives, the need to make a difference in the world, and the need to be of service.

The first three levels focus on our personal self-interest—meeting the needs of the ego. The last three levels focus on the common good—meeting the needs of the soul.

The focus of the fourth level is transformation—a shift from self-interest to the common good. This is where the ego learns to let go of its fears so that it can become one with the soul. Individuals who focus *exclusively* on the satisfaction of the lower needs, tend to live self-centered, shallow lives, subconsciously or consciously dominated by the fears of the ego.

The fears of the ego lead us to believe that we do not have enough of what we need. Consequently, we are never fully happy because we do not have enough money, we do not have enough love, and we do not have enough respect. If we grew up without one, some, or all of these basic needs being satisfied, we find ourselves trying to fill the emptiness we feel inside by getting what we want from the external world. In this situation, we lead a dependency-based existence. We are dependent on others for survival, protection and safety, love, and our sense of self worth. It is only when we release the fears of the ego that keep us in a dependency-based existence that we become free.

Individuals that focus *exclusively* on the satisfaction of the higher needs tend to lack the skills necessary to operate effectively in the physical world. They can be ineffectual and impractical when it comes to taking care of their basic needs. We say they are not "grounded."

To be successful in the world we need to learn how to master the satisfaction of all our needs so we can operate from full-spectrum consciousness. We master level 1 by developing the practical skills that are necessary to ensure our physical survival. We master level 2 by developing the interpersonal relationship skills that are necessary to feel safe and to be loved. We master level 3 by developing the emotional skills that are necessary to feel good about ourselves in all situations—developing a healthy sense of self-esteem.

We master level 4 by learning to release the subconscious and conscious fears we hold about satisfying our personal needs so that we can blend the needs of the ego with the needs of the soul. We shift from "what's in it for me" to "what's best for the common good."

We master level 5 when we discover our personal transcendent meaning for existence. We master level 6 by actualizing our sense of meaning by making a difference in the world. We master level 7 when making a difference becomes a way of life and we embrace the concept of self-less service.

The successful mastery of each stage involves two steps: first, becoming aware of the emergent need, and second, developing the skills that are necessary to satisfy the need. Thus, we are always aware of the needs of the level of consciousness we are operating from and the needs of the previous levels we have passed through, but we are unaware of the needs of the next and subsequent levels of consciousness. We are unconsciously incompetent at the next level of consciousness.

When we first become aware of a need, we are generally unskilled at satisfying it—we are consciously incompetent. As we learn the skills that are necessary to satisfy a need, we become consciously competent. Eventually, when we have mastered the skills that are necessary to satisfy our needs at a particular level of consciousness, we become unconsciously competent at that level. We don't have to think about it anymore. It becomes natural, like driving a car.

The Seven Levels of Group Consciousness

The seven stages in the development of personal consciousness also apply to the development of group consciousness, where "group" is defined as a collection of individuals who share a common physical heritage (culture of blood) or a common purpose (culture of meaning). Included within the definition of "cultures of meaning" are all forms of organizations, such as corporations, government institutions, and nongovernmental organizations (NGOs). Included within the definition of "cultures of blood" are all forms of social units, such as clans, tribes, communities, and nations.

Groups grow and develop in the same way as individuals—by successfully mastering the satisfaction of their needs. The most successful groups are those that develop full-spectrum consciousness—mastery of the needs associated with every level of consciousness. They are able to respond appropriately to all of life's challenges. The seven stages in the development of group consciousness are shown in Table 2–2.

Groups master level 1 by developing skills and competencies to ensure the physical and financial survival of the group. Groups master level 2 by developing skills and abilities to create harmonious relationships that give group members a sense of belonging and mutual protection. Groups master level 3 by creating order through the development of rules, regulations, laws, systems, processes, and structures that allow the group to perform effectively with pride within their framework of their existence.

Groups master level 4 by balancing the needs of the group ego (the interests of the decision-making authority or leadership elite) with the needs of the group members (the collective interest of the group members). The decision-making authority empowers group members by giving them a voice. Without empowerment or participation of group members in decision making, this level of consciousness cannot be

Table 2-2 The Seven Stages/Levels of Group Consciousness

Level	Motivation	Focus
7	Service	Caring for humanity, future generations, and the planet
6	Making a difference	Cooperating with and forming alliances with other groups
5	Internal cohesion	Aligning group members around a shared vision, mission, and values
4	Transformation	Involving group members and giving them a voice in decision making
3	Self-esteem	Creating order, performance, and effectiveness that engenders respect and group pride
2	Relationship	Building harmonious internal relationships that create a sense of belonging
1	Survival	Establishing conditions of financial stability and safety for group members

attained and the shift from a focus on self-interest to focus on the common good cannot occur.

Groups master level 5 by aligning the values and motivations of *all* group members with the vision, mission, and espoused values of the group. This results in internal cohesion and an enhanced capacity for group action. Groups master level 6 by building strategic alliances with other like-minded groups who share similar values, motivations, and aspirations and by deepening the internal connectedness of group members through mentoring, coaching and caring about the personal fulfillment of all members of the group. Groups master level 7 by continuing to deepen the internal connectedness of the group through the exercise of compassion and forgiveness and by expanding the sense of external connectedness by building alliances or collective governance structures with other groups based on a foundation of shared values and a shared vision of the future.

The seven levels of group consciousness is the blueprint that governs the evolution of consciousness of all group forms—both cultures of blood and cultures of meaning. From an evolutionary perspective, the first three levels in the development of group consciousness represent stages in the emergence and development of the group ego (the decision-making authority or leadership elite), and the last three levels represent stages in the emergence and unfolding of the group soul (the collective interest of all group members). Between the last level in the development of the group ego, and the first level in the unfolding of the group soul, lies the fourth level in the development of group consciousness (transformation). This is the level where the group learns to align the needs of its ego with the needs of its soul: the interests of the leadership elite align with the interests of all group members. This is the level of empowerment.

Cultural transformation is never a singular event. It is an ongoing series of encounters between the needs generated by the subconscious fear-based beliefs of the decision-making authority or leadership elite, and the needs of group members. When the members of the leadership elite are focused on satisfying their own self-interests, rather than the needs of the group members, cultural transformation can be very painful. It can involve strikes, insurrection, rebellion, revolution, or even civil war. When the leadership elite start making decisions that focus on the collective interest of the group, rather than their personal self-interests, cultural transformation can proceed relatively easily and smoothly.

The most evolved system for group governance that the human species has devised is called *democracy*. Democracy is a system of governance designed to ensure that the consciousness of the decision-making authority of a group always reflects the consciousness of the group members. If the decision-making authority (elected officials) is out of step with the needs of group members it loses its hold on power by not being reelected. Other officials and leaders whose consciousness is more in alignment with the consciousness of the majority of the group members will replace them.

Groups that operate nondemocratically (institutions and organizations) are more successful when the leader of the group (or the decision-making authority) seeks and acts on the counsel of the group members; in other words, when participation in decision making and/or decision formulation is extended to all group members, and the decisions made by the decision-making authority are in the best interest of all group members.

Groups work best when all members of the group, and all subgroups, share a common vision of the future and operate on the basis of a shared set of values. In such situations, members of the group are able to operate with responsible freedom and decision making can be pushed to the periphery. When values are not shared and leaders operate from self-interest, internal factions develop. This creates internal competition and leads to empire building, information hoarding and blame. In such situations, the self-interest of the leaders can threaten the survival of the group.

With this understanding of the seven levels of personal consciousness and the seven levels of group consciousness, let us now examine how we use the seven levels of consciousness model to develop a cultural diagnostic of an organization using the cultural transformation tools.

3

The Cultural
Transformation Tools

We have been using the cultural transformation tools (CTT) in corporations, government agencies, and nongovernmental organizations since 1997. The cultural transformation tools have also been used in schools, classrooms, religious institutions, and communities. We are currently (2005) pioneering the use of the cultural transformation tools to explore the consciousness of nations. This work will be featured in my upcoming book (2006/2007), *Love, Fear, and the Destiny of Nations: An Exploration of the Role of Business and Government in the Evolution of Human Consciousness.*

The basic technology we use to measure the consciousness of individuals and groups, and the techniques we use to implement cultural transformation, were taught to more than 1,000 consultants and change agents on six continents from 1997 to 2005. In this same period, we mapped the values of more than 500 companies from 35 nations in 18 different languages. The cultural transformation tools are used by some of the most prestigious companies and business consultants in the world.

The success of the CTT is due to their ability to provide a detailed roadmap for the evolution of consciousness of an organization or any group of individuals that share a common heritage or purpose. In some instances, the objective of using the tools is cultural transformation, and in other instances the purpose is to build a values-driven organization. Whatever the purpose, the desired end result is always to build a sustainable high-performance organization that makes the group more "successful" at what they do.

The CTT are used in mergers and acquisitions to guide the successful integration of cultures and for leadership coaching to support leaders and managers in their own personal transformation.

Another reason why the CTT are becoming increasingly popular is that organizations are recognizing that their cultures are a source of competitive advantage. They are devoting more of their resources to implementing cultural transformation programs and values-management (monitoring their cultures). The reason for this is that there is an emerging consensus that

(1) Cultural capital is the new frontier of competitive advantage— it is the key differentiator between a good company and a great company, and between success and failure.

(2) The culture of an organization is a reflection of the consciousness of its leaders. Thus, cultural transformation begins with the personal transformation of the leaders.

(3) Measurement matters: Whatever you focus your intention on, and set targets for, gets done.

We use the CTT cultural values assessment (CVA) to identify and measure the following:

(1) The *personal values* of the individuals who make up the organization

(2) The *values of the current culture* of the organization as perceived by the members of the organization

(3) The *desired culture values* of the organization as expressed by the members of the organization

Measures of the personal consciousness, current culture, and desired culture are obtained for the organization as a whole, and for specified demographic categories. Typical demographic categories include position (leaders, managers, staff), grade, business units, locations, gender, age, ethnicity, length of service, and so forth. The results allow us to measure the alignment of employees' personal values with the values in the current culture of the organization and the alignment of the values in the current culture with the desired culture values.

We can also measure the cultural entropy within any specific demographic grouping. Cultural entropy is defined as *the proportion of energy in a human system (organization) that is consumed by nonproductive activities*. It is a measure of the internal frictions—relationship issues, system problems, and structural misalignments that exist in an organization. This topic is explored in greater depth in the following chapters.

At the heart of the CTT technology is the concept that all values and behaviors can be assigned to one of the seven levels of consciousness. Whatever we focus on in our personal lives is a reflection of our individual consciousness; whatever organizations focus on is a reflection of the collective consciousness of the organization. Therefore, if you can identify the values and behaviors of a group of individuals, you can measure the consciousness of the group by mapping their values to the seven levels of consciousness model. Table 3–1 provides examples of how values/behaviors are mapped to each level of consciousness.

Allocation of Values/Behaviors to Levels of Consciousness

Some values and behaviors arising from the lower levels of consciousness are potentially limiting. Potentially limiting values and behaviors occur when the fear-based beliefs of the egos' of leaders, managers, and

Table 3–1 Allocation of Values/Behaviors to Levels of Consciousness

Level of Consciousness	Motivation	Positive Values/Behaviors (P)	Potentially Limiting Values/Behaviors (L)
7	Service	Social responsibility, future generations, compassion	—
6	Making a difference	Mentoring, volunteer work, environmental awareness	—
5	Internal cohesion	Trust, commitment, honesty, integrity, enthusiasm	—
4	Transformation	Adaptability, continuous learning, accountability	—
3	Self-esteem	Productivity, efficiency, professional growth	Bureaucracy, arrogance, image, information hoarding
2	Relationship	Open communication, customer satisfaction, conflict resolution	Blame, internal competition, rivalry, manipulation
1	Survival	Financial stability, profit, employee health	Control, chaos, caution, job security

employees lead to actions that undermine the common good. At level 4, the leaders, managers, and employees learn to overcome these fears. Consequently, there are no potentially limiting values in the upper levels of consciousness. Thus, we can allocate values/behaviors into two categories—positive (P) and potentially limiting (L).

The values/behaviors listed in Table 3–1 can be further categorized into four value types–individual values (I), relationship values (R), organizational values (O), and societal values (S). Table 3–2 shows examples of how the values/behaviors in Table 3–1 are categorized according to value types and positive and potentially limiting values.

One further values categorization we use is known as the business needs scorecard (BNS). Most of the values/behaviors in Table 3–1 can be categorized into six business categories: finance, fitness (performance-related values), client relations, evolution (ability to create new products and services), culture, and societal contribution. Some values span multiple categories and are therefore not allocated to any one particular category. Table 3–3 shows how the values/behaviors in Table 3–1 are categorized according to the BNS.

The Seven Levels of Organizational Consciousness

In Chapter 2, I described the seven levels of personal consciousness model and the seven levels of group consciousness model. I will now describe the seven levels of organizational consciousness model as it applies to corporations. The seven levels of consciousness of government institutions and nongovernmental organizations are similar to the seven levels of corporate consciousness. The main difference is that the underlying purpose of government institutions and nongovernmental

Table 3–2 Allocation of Values/Behaviors to Value Types and Positive and Potentially Limiting Values

	Individual Values/ Behaviors (I)	Relationship Values/ Behaviors (R)	Organizational Values/ Behaviors (O)	Societal Values/ Behaviors (S)
P O S I T I V E	Adaptability Commitment Honesty Integrity Enthusiasm	Accountability Compassion Conflict resolution Mentoring Open communication Trust Customer satisfaction	Continuous learning Efficiency Financial stability Productivity Professional growth Profit Employee Health	Environmental awareness Future generations Social responsibility Volunteer work
L I M I T I N G	Caution	Arrogance Blame Control Information hoarding Internal competition Manipulation Rivalry	Bureaucracy Chaos Image Job security	—

Table 3-3   Allocation of Values/Behaviors to the Business Needs Scorecard

	Finance	Fitness	Client Relations	Evolution	Culture	Societal Contribution	Not Allocated
P O S I T I V E	Financial stability, Profit	Accountability, Efficiency, Productivity	Customer satisfaction	Adaptability, Continuous learning	Enthusiasm, Open communication, Conflict resolution, Trust, Mentoring	Volunteer work, Environmental awareness, Social responsibility, Future generations	Commitment, Compassion, Honesty, Integrity, Professional growth, Employee health
L I M I T I N G		Bureaucracy, Chaos, Information hoarding, Internal competition, Rivalry, Job security	Image	Caution	Control, Blame, Manipulation	—	Arrogance

organizations is the sustainable delivery of services (mission assurance), not the sustainable delivery of wealth (profit/shareholder value).

Organizations grow and develop in the same way as individuals. They have seven well-defined developmental stages. Each stage focuses on a particular existential need that is common to all human group structures. Organizations develop and grow by learning to master the satisfaction of these needs. Organizations that learn how to master all seven needs operate from full-spectrum consciousness. Our research shows that these are the most resilient and profitable corporations because they have the ability to respond appropriately to all business challenges. The seven levels of organizational consciousness are shown in Figure 3–1.

The "lower" needs, levels 1 to 3, focus on the basic needs of business: the pursuit of profit, satisfying customers, and high-performance systems and processes. The emphasis is on the self-interest of the organization and its shareholders. The "higher" needs, levels 5 to 7, focus on group cohesion, building mutually beneficial alliances and partnerships,

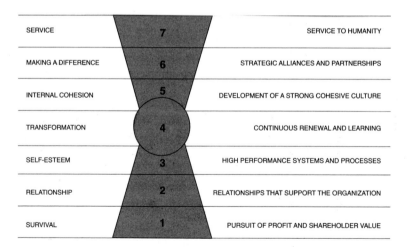

Figure 3–1 Seven Levels of Organizational Consciousness

and the role of the organization in a local and societal context. The emphasis is on enhancing the common good of all stakeholders—employees, customers, and society. The focus of the fourth level is transformation—a shift from fear-based, rigid, authoritarian hierarchies to more open, inclusive, adaptive systems of governance that empower employees to operate with responsible freedom (accountability).

Organizations that focus *exclusively* on the satisfaction of the lower needs are not usually market leaders. They can be successful, but in general they are too internally focused and self-absorbed or too rigid and bureaucratic to be market leaders because they are unable to adapt to changing conditions and do not empower employees. There is little enthusiasm among the work force and innovation and creativity are not nurtured. They are often ruled by fear and are not healthy places to work. Employees often feel frustrated and complain about stress.

Organizations that focus *exclusively* on the satisfaction of the higher needs lack the basic business skills necessary to operate effectively. They are ineffectual and impractical when it comes to financial matters, they are not customer-oriented, and they lack the systems and processes necessary for high performance. They are simply not grounded in the reality of business.

Full-Spectrum Consciousness

To be successful and remain resilient organizations need to learn how to master every level of consciousness.

- They master level 1 by focusing on financial stability and employee safety.
- They master level 2 by focusing on open communication, respect for individuals, and customer satisfaction.

- They master level 3 by focusing on performance, results, and best practices.
- They master level 4 by focusing on adaptability, innovation, employee empowerment, and continuous learning.
- They master level 5 by developing a cohesive culture based on a shared vision and shared values that create an increased capacity for collective action.
- They master level 6 by building strategic alliances with like-minded partners, providing mentoring and coaching for their managers and leaders, and embracing environmental stewardship.
- They master level 7 by focusing on social responsibility, ethics, global thinking, and keeping a long-term perspective on their business and its impact on future generations.

Each of the seven levels of organizational consciousness is explained in more detail below.

Level 1: Survival Consciousness

The first need for an organization is financial survival. Without profits or access to a continuing stream of funds, organizations quickly perish. Every organization needs to make financial stability a primary concern. A precondition for success at this level is a healthy focus on the bottom line. When companies become too entrenched in survival consciousness and have deep-seated insecurities about the future, they develop an unhealthy short-term focus on shareholder value. In such situations, making the quarterly numbers—satisfying the needs of Wall Street—can preoccupy the minds of the leaders to the exclusion of all other factors.

This leads to excessive control, micro-management, caution, and a tendency to be risk-averse. Businesses that operate in this way are not interested in strategic alliances; takeovers are more their game. They will purchase a company and plunder its assets. They see people and the earth as resources to be exploited for gain. When asked to conform to regulations, they do the minimum. They have an attitude of begrudging compliance. Organizations experience their deepest fears at this level of consciousness. The key to success at level 1 is strong financial performance and a focus on employee safety. Without profits, companies cannot invest in their employees, create new products, or build strong relationships with their customers and the local community. Financial stability is the first basic essential for all organizations. Employee health and safety is important because the organization needs to protect its greatest asset.

Level 2: Relationship Consciousness

The second need for an organization is harmonious interpersonal relationships and good internal communications. Without good relationships with employees, customers, and suppliers, company survival is compromised. The critical issue at this level of consciousness is to create a sense of loyalty and belonging among employees and a sense of caring and connection between the organization and its customers. Preconditions for creating a sense of belonging are open communication, mutual respect, and employee recognition. Preconditions for caring are friendliness, responsiveness, and listening. When these are in place, loyalty and satisfaction among employees and customers will be high. Tradition and rituals help cement these bonds. Fears about belonging and lack of respect lead to fragmentation, dissension, and disloyalty. When leaders meet behind closed doors, or fail to communicate openly, employees suspect the worst. Cliques form and gossip becomes rife. When the leaders are more focused on their own success rather than the success of the organization, they begin to compete with each other. When leaders display territorial behaviors, blame, internal competition, and information hoarding become rife, increasing the level of cultural entropy. Family businesses often operate from level 2 consciousness because they are unable to trust outsiders in management positions.

Level 3: Self-Esteem Consciousness

The focus of the third level of organizational consciousness is on performance and measurement. It is about keeping a balanced and watchful eye on all the key operational indicators. At this level of consciousness, the organization is focused on becoming the best it can be through the adoption of best practices and a focus on quality, productivity, and efficiency. Systems and processes are strongly emphasized and strategies are developed to achieve desired results. Reengineering, six sigma, and total quality management are typical responses to issues of performance at this level of consciousness. The critical issue at this level of consciousness is to develop a culture of continuous improvement. A precondition for continuous improvement is the encouragement and reward of excellence. Level 3 organizations tend to be structured hierarchically for the purposes of central control. Top-down is the primary mode of decision making. The hierarchical structure also provides opportunities for rewarding individuals who are focused on their own personal success. Steep hierarchies often serve no other purpose than to cater to managers' needs for recognition, status, and self-esteem. To maintain central control, level 3 organizations develop rules to regulate and bring order to all aspects of their business. Companies that are predominantly focused at this level of consciousness can easily degenerate into power-based silos, rigid authoritarian bureaucracies, and/or a group of internally competitive over achievers. When this happens, failure or collapse will eventually occur unless the organization can switch from being internally focused to externally focused.

Level 4: Transformation Consciousness

The focus of the fourth level of organizational consciousness is on adaptability, employee empowerment, and continuous learning. The critical issue at this level of consciousness is how to stimulate innovation so that new products and services can be developed to respond to market opportunities. This requires the organization to be flexible and take risks. To fully respond to the challenges of this level of consciousness the organization must actively garner employees' ideas and opinions. Everyone must feel that his or her voice is being heard. This requires managers and leaders to admit they do not have all the answers and invite employee participation. For many leaders and managers, this is a new role requiring new skills, which is why it is important to develop the emotional intelligence of managers. They must be able to facilitate high performance in large groups of people who are looking for equality and responsible freedom. Staff want to be held accountable—not micro-managed and supervised every moment of every day. One of the dangers at this level of consciousness is to become overly biased toward consensus. Although some level of consensus is important, ultimately decisions must get made. A precondition for success at this level of consciousness is encouraging all employees to think and act like entrepreneurs. More accountability is given to everyone and structures become less hierarchical. Teamwork is encouraged and more attention is given to personal development and relationship skills. Diversity is seen as a positive asset in exploring new ideas. This shift, which brings responsible freedom and equality to workers, cannot fully achieve the desired results unless all employees and teams share the same sense of direction or purpose. This requires a shift to the fifth level of consciousness.

Level 5: Internal Cohesion Consciousness

The focus at the fifth level of consciousness is on building cultural cohesion and developing a capacity for collective action. For this to happen, leaders and managers must set aside their personal agendas and work for the common good. The critical issue at this level of consciousness is developing a shared vision of the future and a shared set of values. The shared vision clarifies the intentions of the organization and gives employees a unifying purpose and direction. The shared values provide guidance on decision-making. When the values are translated into behaviors, they provide a set of parameters that define the boundaries of responsible freedom. The values and behaviors must be reflected in all the processes and systems of the organization with appropriate consequences for those who are not willing to walk-the-talk. A precondition for success at this level is to build a climate of trust. The prerequisites for trust are fairness, openness and competence. Aligning employees' personal sense of mission with the organization's vision will create a climate of commitment and enthusiasm at all levels of the organization. Personal productivity and creativity increase as individuals align with their passion. In level 5 organizations, failures become lessons, and work becomes fun. The key to success at this level of consciousness is the establishment of a strong, positive, unique cultural identity that differentiates the organization from its competitors. The culture of the organization becomes part of the brand. This is particularly important in service organizations where employees have close contact with customers and the general public. At this and subsequent levels of consciousness, organizations preserve their unique culture by promoting from within.

Level 6: Making a Difference Consciousness

The focus at the sixth level of organizational consciousness is on deepening the level of internal connectedness in the organization and expanding the sense of external connectedness. Internally, the focus is on helping employees find personal fulfillment through their work. Externally, the focus is on building mutually beneficial partnerships and alliances with business partners, the local community, and in certain circumstances with nongovernmental organizations—in other words with all stakeholders. The critical issue at this level of consciousness is that employees and customers see the organization is making a difference in the world, either through its products and services, its involvement in the local community or its willingness to fight for causes that improve the well being of humanity. Employees and customers must feel that the company cares about them and their future. Companies operating at this level of consciousness go the extra mile to make sure they are being responsible citizens. They support and encourage employees' activities in the local community by providing time off for employees to do volunteer work and/or making a financial contribution to the charities in which employees are involved. At this level of consciousness, organizations create an environment were employees can excel. The organization supports employees in becoming all they can become both in terms of their professional *and* their personal growth. Everyone supports everyone else. A precondition for success at this level is developing leaders with a strong sense of empathy. Leaders must recognize that they must not only provide direction for the organization, but they must also become the servants of those who work for them. They must create an

values template, which is used to map the values that are important to employees in their personal lives, and an organizational values template, which is used to map the values of the current and desired culture of the organization. The personal template differs from the organizational template in that it does not contain organizational type values (the types of values listed in column three of Table 3–2). If values like continuous learning and efficiency *are* used on a personal template, they are classified as individual values.

The purpose of the customization is to make sure the values/behaviors that are available for selection correspond not only to the societal culture but also to the culture of the type of organization. For example, the template of personal values we use in Asian countries is different from the template of personal values we use in Europe or North America, particularly with regard to relationship values.

In many parts of Asia, there are strong kinship bonds (level 2) that are reflected in values such as "respect for elders" and "filial duty." These values have practically disappeared from the more independence-based cultures of Europe and North America.

The customization of the organizational template also takes account of the business vernacular, and the vision, mission, and values of the organization. The template must reflect the day-to-day language and concerns of the organization. For example, we would not use the word "profit" in a template for a governmental organization unless this was part of their culture. In the case of businesses that focus on fashion, beauty products, and television companies we would make the value "image" positive, whereas in most organizations "image" is a potentially limiting value. "Image" usually indicates attention is being given to form rather than substance.

Once the personal and organizational templates have been created, and the list of demographic categories has been chosen, we set up a website where employees can log on and take the cultural values assessment. The time it takes to complete a cultural values assessment varies between 15 and 20 minutes.

Employees are first asked to check the demographic categories that apply to them, and then they are asked to answer three questions. The questions usually take the form of the following:

> Which of the following values/behaviors most represent who you are, not what you desire to become? Pick ten (from the Personal Template)
>
> Which of the following values/behaviors most represent how your organization currently operates? Pick ten (from the Organizational Template)
>
> Which of the following values/behaviors most represent how you would like your organization to operate? Pick ten (from the Organizational Template)

The wording of the questions can be amended, but the purpose is always to collect personal values, current culture values, and desired culture values. We can substitute the word "team" for the word "organization" if we want to use the cultural values assessment to identify a team culture.

The results for the group of 53 managers at Flexite are seen in Figures 4–1 to 4–5.

Values Plot

Figure 4–1 shows the top 10 personal values of the group, the top 10 current culture values, and the top 12 desired culture values arranged in order of the number of votes received for each value (the numbers in parenthesis appearing after the value). The values are plotted against the

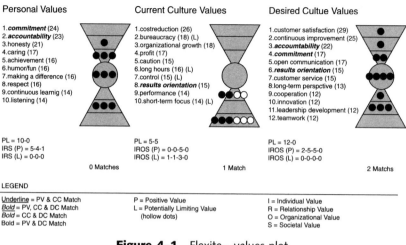

Personal Values | Current Culture Values | Desired Cultue Values

1.**commitment** (24)
2.**accountability** (23)
3.honesty (21)
4.caring (17)
5.achievement (16)
6.humor/fun (16)
7.making a difference (16)
8.respect (16)
9.continuous learnig (14)
10.listening (14)

1.costreduction (26)
2.bureaucracy (18) (L)
3.organizational growth (18)
4.profit (17)
5.caution (15)
6.long hours (16) (L)
7.control (15) (L)
8.**results orientation** (15)
9.performance (14)
10.short-term focus (14) (L)

1.customer satisfaction (29)
2.continuous improvement (25)
3.**accountability** (22)
4.**commitment** (17)
5.open communication (17)
6.**results orientation** (15)
7.customer service (15)
8.long-term perspctive (13)
9.cooperation (12)
10.innovation (12)
11.leadership development (12)
12.teamwork (12)

PL = 10-0
IRS (P) = 5-4-1
IRS (L) = 0-0-0

PL = 5-5
IROS (P) = 0-0-5-0
IROS (L) = 1-1-3-0

PL = 12-0
IROS (P) = 2-5-5-0
IROS (L) = 0-0-0-0

0 Matches | 1 Match | 2 Matchs

LEGEND

Underline = PV & CC Match
Bold = PV, CC & DC Match
Bold = CC & DC Match
Bold = PV & DC Match

P = Positive Value
L = Potentially Limiting Value
   (hollow dots)

I = Individual Value
R = Relationship Value
O = Organizational Value
S = Societal Value

Figure 4–1   Flexite—values plot

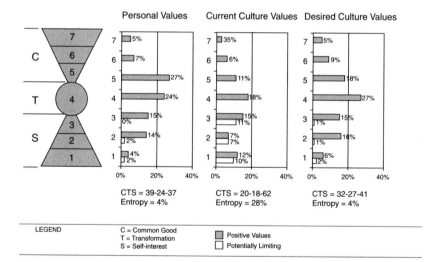

Personal Values | Current Culture Values | Desired Culture Values

7: 5% | 7: 35% | 7: 5%
6: 7% | 6: 6% | 6: 9%
5: 27% | 5: 11% | 5: 8%
4: 24% | 4: 18% | 4: 27%
3: 0% 15% | 3: 15% 11% | 3: 1% 15%
2: 2% 14% | 2: 7% 7% | 2: 1% 16%
1: 4% 2% | 1: 12% 10% | 1: 6% 2%

CTS = 39-24-37
Entropy = 4%

CTS = 20-18-62
Entropy = 28%

CTS = 32-27-41
Entropy = 4%

LEGEND

C = Common Good
T = Transformation
S = Self-interest

▣ Positive Values
☐ Potentially Limiting

Figure 4–2   Flexite—values distribution

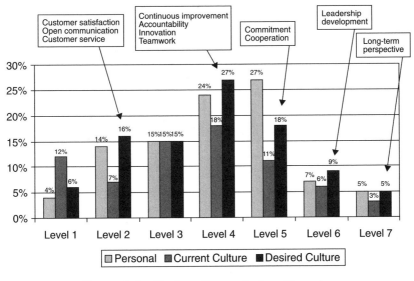

Figure 4-3   Flexite—alignment of positive values

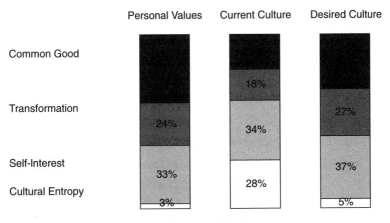

Figure 4-4   Flexite—CTS distribution

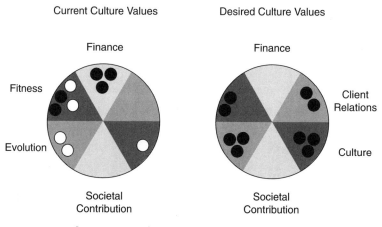

Figure 4–5   Flexite—business needs scorecard

seven levels of consciousness model. Each black dot represents one of the top scoring positive values. Each white dot represents one of the top scoring potentially limiting values. The ratio PL represents the number of positive values (P) compared with the number of potentially limiting values (L) in the top ten. The ratio IROS represents the number of individual (I), relationship (R), organizational (O), and societal values (S) in the top ten (note that there are no organizational values on the personal template, therefore this ratio is represented by IRS).

The top ten personal values of the Flexite managers are distributed across four levels of consciousness, with three values each at level 2 (relationship consciousness), level 4 (transformation consciousness), and level 5 (internal cohesion consciousness). There is one value at level 6 (making a difference consciousness). The level 2 values are caring, respect and listening. The level 4 values are accountability, achievement, and continuous learning. The level 5 values are commitment, honesty and humor/fun. The level 6 value is making a difference. The IRS comprises five individual values, four relationship values and one societal value. All top ten values are positive.

The top ten current culture values as perceived by the Flexite managers are distributed across two levels of consciousness, with six values at level 1 (survival consciousness), and four values at level 3 (self-esteem consciousness). Three of the level 1 values are positive—cost reduction, organizational growth, and profit; and three are potentially limiting—caution, control, and short-term focus. Two of the level 3 values are positive—results orientation and performance; and two are potentially limiting—bureaucracy and long hours. The IROS comprises one potentially limiting individual value—caution; one potentially limiting relationship value—control; and three potentially limiting organizational values—bureaucracy, long hours, and short-term focus. There are five positive organizational values—cost reduction, organizational growth, profit, results orientation, and performance. Altogether, there are five positive values and five potentially limiting values in the top ten.

There are 12 top values in the desired culture because the ninth through twelfth values all scored the same number of votes. All top 12 values are positive. There are three values at level 2—customer satisfaction, open communication, and customer service; one value at level 3—results orientation; four values at level 4—continuous improvement, accountability, innovation, and teamwork; two values at level 5—commitment and cooperation; one value at level 6—leadership development; and one value at level 7—long-term perspective. The IROS comprises two individual values—commitment and innovation; five relationship values—accountability, open communication, cooperation, teamwork, and leadership development; and five organizational values—continuous improvement, results orientation, long-term perspective, customer satisfaction, and customer service.

There are no matching values between the personal and current culture values (these would be underlined values). There is one matching value between the current culture and desired culture (values in bold and italics)—results orientation; and there are two matching values between the personal values and desired culture values (values in bold)—accountability and commitment, neither of which are found in the current culture. There are no values that are common to personal, current culture, and desired culture.

The first thing to note about the Flexite management team is that there is a significant misalignment between their personal values and the values they perceive in the current culture of the organization: There are no matching values. They clearly are having difficulty in bringing their full selves to work. There is also a misalignment between the current culture values and desired culture values with only one matching value. There is a relatively close alignment, in terms of levels of consciousness, between the distribution of the top personal values and the top desired culture values suggesting that they have the capacity to create the culture they want to see.

The key issues for this group of managers are as follows:

Relationship Values

The managers are people-oriented as shown by the high number of relationship values in their personal values (IRS = 5-4-1). There are five relationship values in their desired culture (IROS = 2-5-5-0). There are no positive relationship values in the current culture (IROS [P] = 0-0-5-0) and one potentially limiting relationship value (IROS [L] = 1-1-3-0). The relationship values they want to see more of are accountability, open communication, cooperation, teamwork, and leadership development. A further indication of their need for a focus on relationship values is that they have three values at level 2 (relationship consciousness) in their personal values and in their desired culture. There are no values at level 2 in the current culture.

Inward Looking

The managers see the company as inward looking as shown by: the lack of focus on customer oriented values in the current culture, and the strong focus on bureaucracy. They want the company to become more outward focused as shown by the fact that the number 1 value in the desired culture is customer satisfaction and the number 7 value is customer service.

Fear

The organization is driven by fear and a lack of trust as shown by the values of caution and control. Other symptoms of this fear-based culture are bureaucracy, short-term focus, and long hours.

Bottom-Line Results and Performance

The organization currently focuses almost exclusively on bottom-line results, as shown by cost reduction, organizational growth, profit, and short-term focus, and on performance, as shown by results orientation and performance.

This is a company driven by the stock market with a single focus: how to make more money for its shareholders. They are relatively successful in this pursuit, but find it difficult to keep their talented people because there is no alignment between the personal values of the executives and the current culture. It is not surprising therefore that the senior management is feeling stressed and frustrated.

There is a strong possibility that the company will fail in the long run because of the following:

(1) It is not paying attention to its customers,

(2) It is rigid and bureaucratic, and

(3) It is either unwilling or unable to innovate and think about the long-term.

Flexite is making the classic mistake of milking the cow for all it is worth without any regard for the long-term development of new products or the needs of their customers. Emotional intelligence skills are lacking in the senior management group. They need some form of leadership development program to build a stronger framework of open communication, cooperation, and teamwork.

One of the more positive signs in the values assessment results is that the distribution of the desired culture values is almost full-spectrum. The only missing level is level 1 where the company is already strong. What this suggests is the senior management group knows what to do to make Flexite a top performing company. Furthermore, the relatively strong set of values at levels 4 and 5 in their personal values suggests that given half a chance, they would be able to transform the company.

We always find that the antidotes to the issues found in the current culture are expressed in the desired culture values. Thus, in the case of Flexite, the antidote to bureaucracy is accountability and continuous improvement; the antidote to short-term focus is long-term perspective; and the antidote to caution and control is leadership development with a focus on open communication and teamwork.

Values Distribution

Turning to Figure 4–2, which shows the distribution of all the votes for all values, the most striking feature is the relatively high level of cultural entropy (28%) in the current culture. Cultural entropy is calculated by dividing all the votes for potentially limiting values by the total number

Table 4–1 Significance of Different Levels of Cultural Entropy

Cultural Entropy	Implications
≥40%	Critical Issues—Requiring cultural and structural transformation, selective changes in leadership, leadership mentoring, leadership coaching, and leadership development
30%–39%	Serious Issues—Requiring cultural and structural transformation, leadership mentoring, leadership coaching, and leadership development
20%–29%	Significant Issues—Requiring cultural and structural transformation and leadership coaching
10%–19%	Minor Issues—Requiring cultural and/or structural adjustment
<10%	Prime—Healthy functioning

of votes for all values. Table 4–1 shows the significance of different measures of cultural entropy. These levels of significance have been established experientially by comparing the results of more than 200 organizations. In the case of Flexite, the level of cultural entropy suggests that there are significant issues requiring cultural and structural transformation and leadership coaching. This is in line with the desire of the executive's for leadership development (number 11, Desired Culture Value).

Distribution of Positive Values

Figure 4–3 is the same as Figure 4–2 except the potentially limiting values have been removed and the bar graph is presented vertically rather than horizontally in such a way that we can easily compare the distribution of positive personal, current culture and desired culture votes for each level of consciousness. Let us examine the degree of alignment of each level of consciousness in turn.

We see a strong emphasis at level 1 in the current culture (12%), which is much higher than the personal values and desired culture values. This can be taken as positive and suggests that this organization has mastered level 1. At level 2 we see the reverse. There are 14% and 16% of the votes at level 2 in the personal values and desired culture values, respectively, and only 7% in the current culture. The group would like to see much more emphasis given to this level of consciousness by focusing on values such as open communication, customer satisfaction, and customer service. At level 3 personal, current culture and desired culture are all in balance, suggesting the company has achieved an adequate level of mastery at this level. At level 4, there are 24% and 27% of the votes in the personal values and desired culture, respectively, and only 18% in the current culture. The group would like to see more emphasis given to this level of consciousness and in particular to continuous improvement, accountability, innovation and teamwork. There is also a gap at level 5, where there are 11% of the votes in the current culture and 27% and 18% in the personal values and desired culture respectively. The group would like to see more commitment and cooperation. At level 6 the group wants to see more emphasis on leadership development, and at level 7 they want to see more attention given to the long-term perspective.

CTS Chart

Figure 4–4 shows the CTS ratio (Common good, Transformation, Self-interest), which is arrived at by the addition of the percentage of votes for the three higher levels of consciousness (C), the percentage of votes at level 4 (T), and the addition of the percentage of votes for the three lower levels of consciousness (S). There is a reasonably strong alignment between this group's personal values and their desired culture values. The personal ratio is 39-24-37 compared to the desired culture ratio of 32-27-41. The CTS ratio for the current culture (20-18-62) shows only 20% of votes for the common good, 18% for transformation and 62% for self-interest. This suggests that the senior executives in this group operate from fear and are focused on serving their own needs. This is underlined by the atypically high percentage of potentially limiting values (4%) in the personal values and in the desired culture. Some of the senior people in this group cannot get past the need for control.

Business Needs Scorecard

Figure 4–5 shows the allocation of the top current and desired culture values to the six categories of the business needs scorecard. The six categories are as follows:

(1) Finance: Values and behaviors that have an impact on the bottom line such as cost reduction, profit, financial stability, and so forth.

(2) Fitness: Values and behaviors that have an impact on performance such as productivity, efficiency, accountability, quality, and so forth.

(3) Client relations: Values and behaviors that have an impact on client relationships such as customer satisfaction, customer collaboration, client focus, and so forth.

(4) Evolution: Values and behaviors that have an impact on the development of new products or services such as innovation, creativity, risk-taking, and so forth.

(5) Culture: Values and behaviors that have an impact on the culture of the organization such as honesty, open communication, trust, commitment, and so forth.

(6) Societal contribution: Values and behaviors that have an impact on the relationship of the organization to the local community or society at large such as environmental awareness, community involvement, human rights, and so forth.

The results for Flexite clearly show that the current focus of the organization is on making money and high performance. *Finance* has three positive values—profit, organizational growth, and cost reduction. *Fitness* has two positive values—results orientation and performance. There are two potentially limiting values that inhibit fitness—bureaucracy and long hours and there are two potentially limiting values—caution and short-term focus, which inhibit the future evolution of the company. The value of control shows up as a potentially limiting value in the category of *culture*.

The desired culture shows a significant shift in emphasis: three positive values in the category of *evolution* (continuous improvement, innovation, and long-term perspective); three positive values in the category of *culture* (commitment, open communication, and cooperation); and two positive values in the category of *client relations* (customer satisfaction and customer service). Because the company has mastered making money there are no values showing up in the desired culture in the category of *finance*. There is no focus on *societal contribution* in the current or desired culture.

The results shown in Figure 4–5 corroborate the earlier findings that this company is not thinking about its future, its clients or its employees. It is on the road to failure unless it can turn the thinking of the leadership group around and remove the fear and self-interest that drives the short-term focus.

Other Examples of the Use of Cultural Transformation Tools Assessment Instruments

The preceding example demonstrates the power of the cultural values assessment (CVA) instrument in providing a detailed diagnostic of the culture of an organization. With this diagnostic, organizations are able to manage their values and adjust their cultural, structural or leadership development programs on an annual basis so they can respond precisely to the evolving needs of the organization. We have found that as the current culture changes, the desired culture also changes, until it eventually reaches a point where there are eight or nine matching values between the top ten current culture values and the top ten desired culture values, and the current culture values are distributed across all levels of consciousness—full-spectrum consciousness.

The Methodist Hospital

One organization that has used the cultural values assessment (CVA) instruments to support its cultural transformation is a high-performing hospital system based in Houston, Texas that has over 7,000 employees. Figure 4–6 shows how the current culture of this organization has evolved over a 3-year period from 2001 to 2003.

What we see in this example is the gradual, year-by-year, progression to full-spectrum consciousness. In 2001, 1,695 employees participated in the cultural values assessment. The results showed five matching values between the current and desired culture (values in bold and italics) and three matching personal and current culture values (values underlined). The top values were spread over four levels. Half the top ten values are situated at level 4 consciousness, indicating an openness to transformation. There was one potentially limiting value in the current culture—

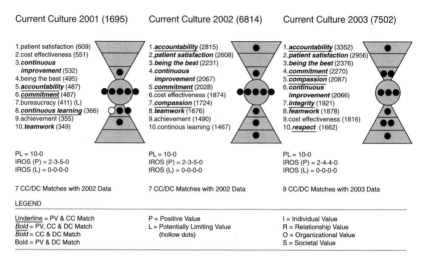

Current Culture 2001 (1695)   Current Culture 2002 (6814)   Current Culture 2003 (7502)

1.patient satisfaction (609)
2.cost effectiveness (551)
3.*continuous*
   improvement (532)
4.being the best (495)
5.*accountability* (487)
6.*commitment* (487)
7.bureaucracy (411) (L)
8.*continuous learning* (366)
9.achievement (355)
10.*teamwork* (349)

1.*accountability* (2815)
2.*patient satisfaction* (2608)
3.*being the best* (2231)
4.*continuous*
   improvement (2067)
5.*commitment* (2028)
6.cost effectiveness (1874)
7.*compassion* (1724)
8.*teamwork* (1676)
9.achievement (1490)
10.continous learning (1467)

1.*accountability* (3352)
2.*patient satisfaction* (2956)
3.*being the best* (2376)
4.*commitment* (2270)
5.*compassion* (2087)
6.*continuous*
   improvement (2066)
7.*integrity* (1921)
8.*teamwork* (1878)
9.cost effectiveness (1816)
10.*respect* (1662)

PL = 10-0
IROS (P) = 2-3-5-0
IROS (L) = 0-0-0-0

PL = 10-0
IROS (P) = 2-3-5-0
IROS (L) = 0-0-0-0

PL = 10-0
IROS (P) = 2-4-4-0
IROS (L) = 0-0-0-0

7 CC/DC Matches with 2002 Data

7 CC/DC Matches with 2002 Data

9 CC/DC Matches with 2003 Data

LEGEND

Underline = PV & CC Match	P = Positive Value	I = Individual Value
Bold = PV, CC & DC Match	L = Potentially Limiting Value	R = Relationship Value
Bold = CC & DC Match	(hollow dots)	O = Organizational Value
Bold = PV & DC Match		S = Societal Value

Figure 4–6   Methodist Hospital—journey to full-spectrum

bureaucracy. A year later, after the implementation of a program of values awareness for employees, there were seven matching current and desired culture values and no potentially limiting values in the list of the top ten current culture values. Again, there were three matching personal and current culture values. The values were spread over six levels of consciousness—almost full-spectrum, with a strong focus at the transformation level. In 2003, the number of matching current and desired culture values increased from seven to nine, and the number of matching personal and current culture values increased from three to five. The level of cultural entropy in 2003 was 13%—a relatively low level indicating only some minor issues.

One of the impacts of the values initiative in this hospital was a reduction in turnover from 24% in 2002 to 15% in 2004, a 38% decline. Vacancy rates went from 6.7% to 3.1% over the same period.[1] The

[1] *Workforce Management*. True Believers at Methodist Hospital by Mathew Gilbert, February 2005, pp. 67–69.

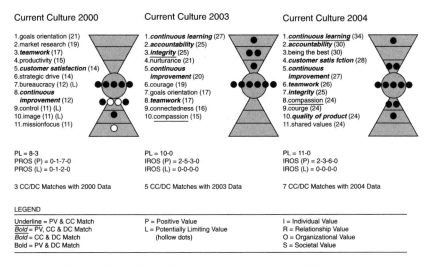

Figure 4–7 HearthStone Homes—journey to full-spectrum

Methodist Hospital has been named as one of the top 100 hospitals in the United States by *U.S. News & World Report*, and one of the top 15 teaching hospitals by Solucient, a benchmarking company.

HearthStone Homes

In another example (Figure 4–7), we see how the culture of a small building company of approximately 100 people based in Nebraska evolved from 2000 to 2004. What is interesting about this example is that the current culture tracks almost precisely the evolution of the personal consciousness of the leader. The chief executive officer (CEO) of this company went through several significant personal transformation experiences between 2000 and 2004. This is reflected in the current culture of the company as shown in Figure 4–7.

Again, we see in this example a gradual, year-by-year, progression to full-spectrum consciousness. In 2000, the results showed three matching values between the current and desired culture. There were no matching personal and current culture values. The top 11 values were spread over the lower four levels of consciousness. Half the top ten values are situated at level 4, consciousness, indicating an openness to transformation. There were three potentially limiting values—bureaucracy, control, and image. Three years later, there was a dramatically different result. The top ten values were spread over the upper four levels of consciousness. There were five matching current and desired culture values, two matching personal and current culture values, and six values situated at the level of transformation. There were no potentially limiting values.

As already indicated, the reason for this reversal was the shift in consciousness of the CEO. During this period the company adopted five values—continuous learning, courage, integrity, nurturance, and spirituality. Spirituality was defined by the following statement: "We honor our connectedness to each other and practice the principles of compassion, generosity, and service which help us to define who we and what we contribute." Each of these values and their accompanying definitions are read aloud at the start of every meeting and the significance of the values with regard to the purpose of the meeting is discussed. The decision made during the meeting must align with the values.

By 2004, the number of matching current and desired culture values increased to seven and the number of matching personal and current culture values increased to three. There were still five values at level 4 consciousness, but now the remaining values were more equally distributed over the lower and upper levels of consciousness. The distribution of top ten current culture values was gradually approaching full-spectrum consciousness. In 2004 the level of cultural entropy was 14%—a relatively low level indicating some minor issues.

Australia New Zealand Bank

Let us consider one more example of a values journey, this time involving a major bank in Australia with over 27,000 employees. When we mapped the values of the organization in 2000, the share price was languishing at A$9.02, of which A$4.04 could be attributed to the intangible assets such as culture. By 2003, the share price was A$18.30, of which A$10.98 could be attributed to the intangible assets. The average compound growth rate of the share price between 1998 and 2003 was 54%. During this same period net profit jumped from just over A$ 1 billion to A$ 2.4 billion. Meanwhile employee satisfaction grew from just under 50% to 82%. A significant reason for this change in performance was the company's values-driven approach to cultural transformation.

Figure 4–8 shows the shift in top ten current culture values over the 4-year period of 2000 to 2003. In 2000, there was one potentially limiting value in the top ten current culture values—bureaucracy. By 2002, this value had dropped out of the top ten. During the first year of the cultural transformation program accountability jumped from number 5 to number 3 and customer focus jumped from number 7 to number 4. By 2002, community involvement entered the top ten current culture

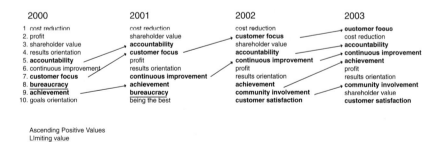

Ascending Positive Values
Limiting value

Figure 4–8   ANZ (Australia New Zealand Bank) values journey—
top ten current culture values

values. In the space of a year, it jumped from number 20 to number 9. By 2003, customer focus was the number 1 value having displaced cost reduction. Accountability was the number 3 value and continuous improvement had gradually moved up from number 7 to number 4. Customer satisfaction entered the top ten at number 10 in 2002 and maintained this position in 2003. What we see in this example is a gradual reordering of the top current culture values with a parallel positive shift in the key indicators of performance.

Small United States Bank

Finally, let us take a look at the example of a small bank in the United States. This assessment was one of the significant milestones in the proof of concept of the CTT. When we measured the culture of this bank in 1998–1 year after bringing CT Tools to the market place—we were pleased to find a real life example of full-spectrum consciousness. Before this time, we were like scientists who had developed a theory that predicted a certain outcome, and we were looking for evidence to prove the theory. We knew full-spectrum current culture consciousness was rare and that an organization that displayed full-spectrum current culture consciousness would have exemplary operating results. Subsequently, we discovered several more examples. Now we come across full-spectrum organizations two or three times a year. Figure 4–9 shows the results of the values of assessment we did for this small United States bank in 1998.

The first point to notice about this values plot is that there is a strong alignment between personal values, current culture values, and desired cultural values. There are three matching personal and current culture values—commitment, integrity, and friendliness (underlined values). There are eight matching current and desired culture values—customer service, teamwork, customer satisfaction, community involvement,

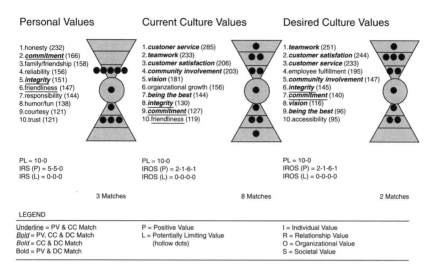

Personal Values

1.honesty (232)
2.*commitment* (166)
3.family/friendship (158)
4.reliability (156)
5.*integrity* (151)
6.friendliness (147)
7.responsibility (144)
8.humor/fun (138)
9.courtesy (121)
10.trust (121)

PL = 10-0
IRS (P) = 5-5-0
IRS (L) = 0-0-0

3 Matches

Current Culture Values

1.*customer service* (285)
2.*teamwork* (233)
3.*customer satisfaction* (206)
4.*community involvement* (203)
5.*vision* (181)
6.organzational growth (156)
7.*being the best* (144)
8.*integrity* (130)
9.*commitment* (127)
10.friendliness (119)

PL = 10-0
IROS (P) = 2-1-6-1
IROS (L) = 0-0-0-0

8 Matches

Desired Culture Values

1.*teamwork* (251)
2.*customer satisfation* (244)
3.*customer service* (233)
4.employee fulfillment (195)
5.*community involvement* (147)
6.*integrity* (145)
7.*commitment* (140)
8.*vision* (116)
9.*being the best* (96)
10.accessibility (95)

PL = 10-0
IROS (P) = 2-1-6-1
IROS (L) = 0-0-0-0

2 Matches

LEGEND

Underline = PV & CC Match	P = Positive Value	I = Individual Value
Bold = PV, CC & DC Match	L = Potentially Limiting Value	R = Relationship Value
Bold = CC & DC Match	(hollow dots)	O = Organizational Value
Bold = PV & DC Match		S = Societal Value

Figure 4–9   Small bank—Full-spectrum organization

vision, being the best, integrity, and commitment (values in bold and italics); and integrity and commitment appear on all three top ten lists of values. Only two of the desired culture values do not appear in the top ten of the current culture—employee fulfillment and accessibility. The second point to notice is that there is full-spectrum consciousness in the current culture and almost full spectrum consciousness in the desired culture.

When we examined the performance of the bank we found the following facts. The bank had record annual profits over the previous 13 years. The average annual growth in the share price from 1993 to 1998 was over 35%. The bank had grown from 1 to 33 locations in 27 years. All staff shares in the profits. Normal profit sharing was approximately 9.5% of base salary, and salaries in the bank were 18.5% above the industry norm.

When we asked the leaders of the bank to tell us how they had built such a successful culture, they told us that their primary concern was employee fulfillment. They believe employee fulfillment leads to customer satisfaction, and if customers are satisfied then shareholder value will increase. So, how does this bank create employee fulfillment? They give bank tellers a sense of their importance by calling them front-line managers. They are trained to handle any inquiry. They provide training for everyone; both personal growth and professional training, with a particular focus on leaders and their development. Even though employee fulfillment was one of the desired culture values that did not appear in the top ten current culture values, it is clear that employees hold the company in high regard. In 2005, this bank took its place in the top half of Fortune Magazine's 100 Best Companies to Work for in America.

Conclusions

What we have learned from these examples, and dozens of other interactions with organizations, can be summarized as follows:

(1) Organizational culture is the new frontier of competitive advantage, particularly in circumstances where talent is in short supply. Talented people will always gravitate to companies that care about their employees and their customers.

(2) Organizational cultures can be changed either by changing the leader, and/or through whole-system change—the topic of a subsequent chapter. Failing companies tend to bring in a new leader from the outside with a different consciousness and different priorities. Successful companies, on the other hand, tend to promote from within so they can preserve their winning culture.

(3) The intangible assets of an organization, such as culture, have a significant impact on the share price of a company. The

intangibles can represent as much as 65% to 85% of a company's stock price. Therefore, one of the ways to improve your share price is to focus on improving the culture.

(4) Whatever you focus on and measure gets done. Many of the organizations using the CTT manage their values by measuring their performance annually against specific targets, such as reducing the number of potentially limiting values, reducing the level of cultural entropy, and increasing the number of matching current and desired culture values. These targets can be set for the company as a whole as well as for each business unit, office or factory location and each functional team. In this way, individual leaders, managers and supervisors can be held accountable for the culture of their units. We have found that even within a strongly positive culture, like The Methodist Hospital in Houston, individual units can display high levels of cultural entropy due to the lack of leadership skills of the manager.

Ultimately, the culture of an organization is a reflection of the personality of the leader or the personalities of the leadership group. Therefore, organizational transformation always begins with the personal transformation of the leaders. Individual values assessments (see Chapter 5) and leadership values assessments (see Chapter 7) play a significant role in helping leaders to change their behaviors.

Full-spectrum consciousness is the natural pathway to long-term success. Time after time, we see groups of employees select desired cultures that have positive values at every level of consciousness or six out of the seven levels (see the Flexite example). We found from our research early on, that full-spectrum organizations are the most successful. What we did not know is that the values that correspond to full-spectrum consciousness, and a fully balanced business needs scorecard, are instinctively chosen by large diverse groups of employees as the healthiest natural state for their organization. When employees go on line and select ten values that represent how they want their organization to operate, they do so independently without referencing each other's choices. They do not consciously collude to choose values that represent full-spectrum consciousness. What we now understand is that there is a natural propensity for groups of people to choose values that collectively exhibit full-spectrum consciousness. This finding is consistent with the theory of the wisdom of crowds.[2]

---

[2] James Surowiecki. *The Wisdom of Crowds.* New York: Doubleday, 1994.

5

Mapping the Values of Individuals

Individual Values Assessments

One of the best ways of raising the awareness of the members of the leadership group to the importance of values alignment is to provide them with their own personal profiles from the cultural values assessment. They are able to see, first hand, their own top personal values, the values they see in the organization, and the values they would like to see in the organization. They are also able to compare their results with the overall results of the leadership group. This can be particularly meaningful when the individual's results differ significantly from the group as a whole. When this occurs, it either means that this individual is the "truth-teller" of the group or it may be indicative of a lack of cultural fit. In either case it may be time for the individual to reflect on his or her future in the organization and may give cause to consider moving on. Conversely, when there is a high degree of alignment, the individual can put aside any doubts that he or she may have about how they fit into the company.

The individual profile when used on its own for coaching purposes is called an individual values assessment (IVA). The survey process is similar to that described in Chapter 4. An individual goes online

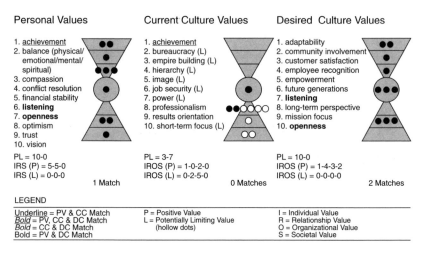

Personal Values

1. achievement
2. balance (physical/
   emotional/mental/
   spiritual)
3. compassion
4. conflict resolution
5. financial stability
6. **listening**
7. **openness**
8. optimism
9. trust
10. vision

PL = 10-0
IRS (P) = 5-5-0
IRS (L) = 0-0-0

1 Match

Current Culture Values

1. achievement
2. bureaucracy (L)
3. empire building (L)
4. hierarchy (L)
5. image (L)
6. job security (L)
7. power (L)
8. professionalism
9. results orientation
10. short-term focus (L)

PL = 3-7
IROS (P) = 1-0-2-0
IROS (L) = 0-2-5-0

0 Matches

Desired Culture Values

1. adaptability
2. community involvement
3. customer satisfaction
4. employee recognition
5. empowerment
6. future generations
7. **listening**
8. long-term perspective
9. mission focus
10. **openness**

PL = 10-0
IROS (P) = 1-4-3-2
IROS (L) = 0-0-0-0

2 Matches

LEGEND

<u>Underline</u> = PV & CC Match	P = Positive Value	I = Individual Value
<u>**Bold**</u> = PV, CC & DC Match	L = Potentially Limiting Value	R = Relationship Value
Bold = CC & DC Match	(hollow dots)	O = Organizational Value
Bold = PV & DC Match		S = Societal Value

Figure 5–1   Robert's values plot

and picks ten values/behaviors that represent who they are; ten values/
behaviors that describe how their organization operates, and ten
values/behaviors that describe how they would like the organization to
operate. Here are four examples of IVA profiles.

Robert

Robert's results (Figures 5–1 and 5–2) are typical of a people-oriented
person (IRS [P] = 5-5-0)[1] working in a power-driven organization. Even
though Robert is driven to find personal success through achievement,
his personal values contain five relationship values—compassion, conflict resolution, listening, openness, and trust. This is a self-actualized
individual who operates from close to full-spectrum consciousness. He
has a potential blind spot in the area of self-esteem consciousness. His
organization is nowhere near full-spectrum. Robert sees seven poten-

[1] More than three relationship values in the IRS suggests a focus on people.

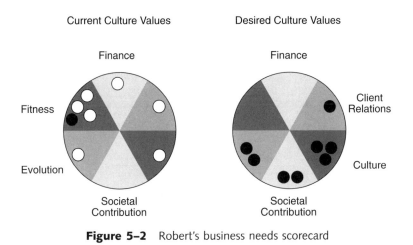

Figure 5–2   Robert's business needs scorecard

tially limiting values in the culture, two of which are relationship values and five of which are organizational values (IROS [L] = 0-2-5-0). These results show that Robert has a weak level of alignment with the culture of the organization—no matching personal and current culture values and only one matching current and desired culture value. For someone like Robert, this is a tough place to work. The only value that Robert has in common with his organization is the drive for achievement.

Robert would like to see two of his personal relationship values given more emphasis in the culture—listening and openness. Openness is a response to the silo-driven mentality that comes with hierarchy and empire building. In addition, Robert wants to replace the bureaucracy with adaptability. He also wants to replace power with empowerment. He understands the importance of focusing on people—customers, employees, and the community. None of these things will happen until this organization develops a much stronger level 2 consciousness.

The business needs scorecard (BNS) supports this analysis. Almost all of the desired culture values are located in the areas of client relations,

Personal Values   Current Culture Values   Desired Culture Values

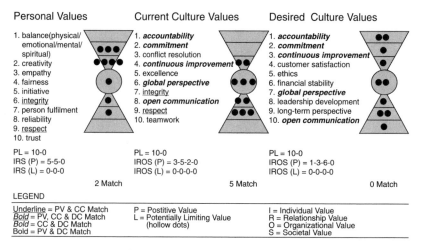

Personal Values	Current Culture Values	Desired Culture Values
1. balance(physical/ emotional/mental/ spiritual) 2. creativity 3. empathy 4. fairness 5. initiative 6. <u>integrity</u> 7. person fulfilment 8. reliability 9. <u>respect</u> 10. trust	1. *accountability* 2. *commitment* 3. conflict resolution 4. *continuous improvement* 5. excellence 6. *global perspective* 7. <u>integrity</u> 8. *open communication* 9. <u>respect</u> 10. teamwork	1. *accountability* 2. *commitment* 3. *continuous improvement* 4. customer satisfaction 5. ethics 6. financial stability 7. *global perspective* 8. leadership development 9. long-term perspective 10. *open communication*
PL = 10-0 IRS (P) = 5-5-0 IRS (L) = 0-0-0	PL = 10-0 IROS (P) = 3-5-2-0 IROS (L) = 0-0-0-0	PL = 10-0 IROS (P) = 1-3-6-0 IROS (L) = 0-0-0-0
2 Match	5 Match	0 Match

LEGEND

<u>Underline</u> = PV & CC Match *Bold* = PV, CC & DC Match *Bold* = CC & DC Match Bold = PV & DC Match	P = Postitive Value L = Potentially Limiting Value (hollow dots)	I = Individual Value R = Relationship Value O = Organizational Value S = Societal Value

Figure 5–3   Sheila's values plot

culture, evolution, and societal contribution—people aspects of the scorecard whereas the current culture shows regression in all these areas of the scorecard except societal contribution.

Sheila

Sheila is another people-oriented person. Unlike Robert, she is working in a people-oriented culture (Figures 5–3 and 5–4). Sheila's personal values show an IRS [P] of 5-5-0 and the current culture of her company show an IROS [P] of 3-5-2-0. Sheila's strong relationship values are matched by the strong relationship values in the organization. Sheila's personal values suggest someone who is approaching self-actualization with either a potential blind spot or unconscious competence at level 1. Level 7 is the next arena of growth for Sheila. Sheila shares two personal values with the organization—integrity and respect. She also has five

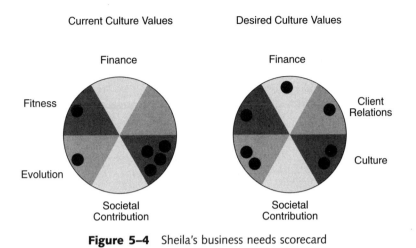

Figure 5–4   Sheila's business needs scorecard

matching current and desired culture values. Sheila has a strong level of
alignment with the culture of the organization.

Despite the positive alignment, Sheila wants to see some changes. She
is looking for a shift to full-spectrum consciousness with an almost fully
balanced BNS. According to Sheila, the organization is currently lacking
focus on customers, ethics, financial stability, a long-term perspective,
and leadership development. Sheila has the insights necessary to build a
full-spectrum high-performance organization.

John

John shares three personal values with the current culture of the
organization—adaptability, experience, and humor/fun. He also has
four matching current and desired culture values (Figures 5–5 and 5–6).
Humor/fun appears in all three lists. This suggests John has a strong
degree of values alignment with his organization. There is an 80%

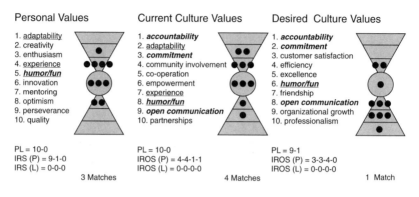

Personal Values

1. adaptability
2. creativity
3. enthusiasm
4. experience
5. *humor/fun*
6. innovation
7. mentoring
8. optimism
9. perseverance
10. quality

PL = 10-0
IRS (P) = 9-1-0
IRS (L) = 0-0-0
3 Matches

Current Culture Values

1. *accountability*
2. adaptability
3. *commitment*
4. community involvement
5. co-operation
6. empowerment
7. experience
8. *humor/fun*
9. *open communication*
10. partnerships

PL = 10-0
IROS (P) = 4-4-1-1
IROS (L) = 0-0-0-0
4 Matches

Desired Culture Values

1. *accountability*
2. *commitment*
3. customer satisfaction
4. efficiency
5. excellence
6. *humor/fun*
7. friendship
8. *open communication*
9. organizational growth
10. professionalism

PL = 9-1
IROS (P) = 3-3-4-0
IROS (L) = 0-0-0-0
1 Match

LEGEND

Underline = PV & CC Match	P = Positive Value	I = Individual Value
Bold = PV, CC & DC Match	L = Potentianlly Limiting Value	R = Relationship Value
Bold = CC & DC Match	(hollow dots)	O = organizational Value
Bold = PV & DC Match		S = Societal Value

Figure 5–5   John's values plot

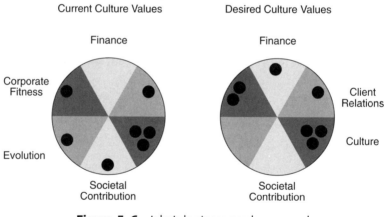

Current Culture Values

Finance

Corporate
Fitness

Evolution

Societal
Contribution

Desired Culture Values

Finance

Client
Relations

Culture

Societal
Contribution

Figure 5–6   John's business needs scorecard

alignment between John's personal levels of consciousness and the current culture of the organization, but only a 50% alignment between the current and desired levels of consciousness.

Even though John feels strongly aligned with the current culture, he wants to see a downshifting or backfilling of values in the desired culture. For him, the organization is not grounded enough at levels 1, 2, and 3. He wants more focus on organizational growth at level 1; more focus on customer satisfaction and friendship at level 2 (open communication is a matching level 2 value in the current and desired culture); and more focus on efficiency, excellence, and professionalism at level 3.

The BNS reflects this situation. The values in the current culture are focused in the lower half of the scorecard: evolution, culture and societal contribution, whereas the values in desired culture are focused in the upper half of the scorecard—finance, fitness and client relationships—the arenas of basic business. The focus on culture is the same in both the current and desired BNS.

When an organizational culture is too focused in the higher levels of consciousness, cultural transformation involves developing stronger systems and processes and giving more attention to finances and money. This situation is often found in not-for-profit organizations or organizations that are more focused on purpose than shareholder returns.

Eric

Eric shows an 80% alignment between personal and current culture levels of consciousness, but has no matching values, and an 80% alignment of current and desired culture levels of consciousness with four matching values (Figures 5–7 and 5–8). Creativity, which is one of Eric's personal values, is not found in the current culture but is emphasized in the desired culture.

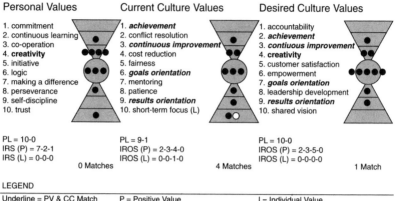

Personal Values

1. commitment
2. continuous learning
3. co-operation
4. **creativity**
5. initiative
6. logic
7. making a difference
8. perseverance
9. self-discipline
10. trust

PL = 10-0
IRS (P) = 7-2-1
IRS (L) = 0-0-0
                    0 Matches

Current Culture Values

1. *achievement*
2. conflict resolution
3. *continuous improvement*
4. cost reduction
5. fairness
6. *goals orientation*
7. mentoring
8. patience
9. *results orientation*
10. short-term focus (L)

PL = 9-1
IROS (P) = 2-3-4-0
IROS (L) = 0-0-1-0
                    4 Matches

Desired Culture Values

1. accountability
2. *achievement*
3. *contiuous improvement*
4. creativity
5. customer satisfaction
6. empowerment
7. *goals orientation*
8. leadership development
9. *results orientation*
10. shared vision

PL = 10-0
IROS (P) = 2-3-5-0
IROS (L) = 0-0-0-0
                    1 Match

LEGEND

Underline = PV & CC Match	P = Positive Value	I = Individual Value
Bold = PV, CC & DC Match	L = Potentially Limiting Value	R = Relationship Value
Bold = CC & DC Match	(hollow dots)	O = Organizational Value
Bold = PV & DC Match		S = Societal Value

Figure 5–7   Eric's values plot

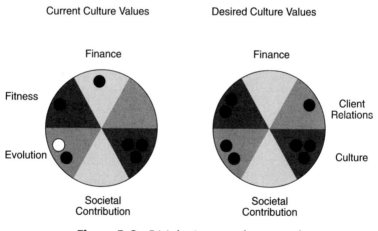

Current Culture Values

Finance

Fitness

Evolution

Societal
Contribution

Desired Culture Values

Finance

Client
Relations

Culture

Societal
Contribution

Figure 5–8   Eric's business needs scorecard

This organization is performance-driven (achievement, continuous improvement, goals orientation, and results orientation) while at the same time emphasizing relationship values (conflict resolution, fairness, and patience). There is also a focus on the bottom line as shown by "cost reduction."

Eric wants to see the organization give up its "short-term focus" and develop a long-term "shared vision." He wants to see more focus on customers and to see employees become more empowered and accountable. For him, these three factors are a consequence of the lack of leadership. He wants more emphasis given to leadership development. The BNS suggests that Eric wants to see more focus on client relations, evolution and fitness. The focus on culture is the same in both the current and desired BNSs.

Conclusions

The IVA is an invaluable coaching instrument. It helps people understand with clarity what is working and not working for them in the culture of their organization and clarifies individuals' feelings about the organization. One of the phrases we often hear when giving the feedback from the IVA is "I thought I was the problem. I knew I didn't fit in, but I didn't know why. Now, I understand it is not me. I am OK. It is the culture that is the problem." The gap between the current and desired culture values enables people to see what is working and not working for them and what they would like to do about it. The gap between personal values and current culture tells an individual to what degree he or she can bring his or her whole self to work.

6

Merging Cultures and the Importance of the Values of the Leadership Group

The main reason for merger disappointment or failure is the lack of an integration strategy or a failure to appreciate the difficulties of merging two different cultures. Fusing the formal systems, such as accounts, payroll, and financial reporting, has its difficulties, but these pale in comparison with the problem of integrating cultures. Merging organizations always employ experts to do a financial due diligence report before the merger; they almost never do a cultural due diligence report. What the acquiring organization often fails to recognize is that if the cultures cannot be integrated, the chances of financial success are minimal.

Mergers that occur between companies with similar values and levels of organizational consciousness have the greatest chance of success. The next most successful mergers are those that involve higher level cultures taking over lower level cultures. In such situations, the benefits of shifting to a higher level culture will be attractive to most employees in the acquired organization but may bring consternation to some managers who operate from the lower levels of consciousness or find it difficult to come to terms with being more open with their employees and inviting them to participate in decision making. With coaching, training, and personal growth seminars, some managers may be able to shift their values and beliefs to align with the higher culture. Others will never make it and will eventually leave. The least successful takeovers are those that involve companies that operate from lower levels of consciousness taking over companies that operate from higher levels of consciousness.[1] These often fail.

The following examples illustrate the use of the cultural transformation tools (CTT) in developing an integration strategy for the merger of two cultures. The survey process is similar to the Flexite example described in Chapter 4. The only significant difference is that a single template of values is customized for both companies, which ensures we are comparing like with like. Once the personal and current culture and desired culture values of both companies have been mapped, we then compare both sets of personal values, both sets of current culture values, and both sets of desired culture values. If there are significant differences in the current and desired cultures, we also compare the desired culture of the company being acquired with the current culture of the company doing the takeover.

Merger 1: Company A and Company B

My first example is not a takeover, but a merger of equals. This is important to note. Merger 1 involves Company A and Company B. A comparison of the personal values, current culture values, and desired culture values of Company A and Company B are shown in Figures 6–1 to 6–6.

The comparison of personal values of employees (Figure 6–1) shows significant similarities. There are eight matching values and both sets of

[1] Richard Barrett. *Liberating the Corporate Soul: Building a Visionary Organization*. Boston: Butterworth-Heinemann; 1998; pp. 95–98.

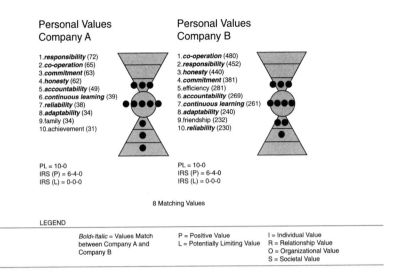

Personal Values
Company A

1.*responsibility* (72)
2.*co-operation* (65)
3.*commitment* (63)
4.*honesty* (62)
5.*accountability* (49)
6.*continuous learning* (39)
7.*reliability* (38)
8.*adaptability* (34)
9.family (34)
10.achievement (31)

PL = 10-0
IRS (P) = 6-4-0
IRS (L) = 0-0-0

Personal Values
Company B

1.*co-operation* (480)
2.*responsibility* (452)
3.*honesty* (440)
4.*commitment* (381)
5.efficiency (281)
6.*accountability* (269)
7.*continuous learning* (261)
8.*adaptability* (240)
9.friendship (232)
10.*reliability* (230)

PL = 10-0
IRS (P) = 6-4-0
IRS (L) = 0-0-0

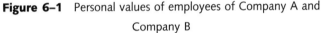

8 Matching Values

LEGEND

Bold+Italic = Values Match between Company A and Company B	P = Positive Value L = Potentially Limiting Value	I = Individual Value R = Relationship Value O = Organizational Value S = Societal Value

Figure 6–1 Personal values of employees of Company A and
Company B

employees have the same IRS (individual, relationship, and societal values; 6-4-0) showing an above-average focus on relationship values.[2] The distribution diagram (Figure 6–2) shows that the employees of Company A operate from a slightly higher level of consciousness than those of Company B. The CTS (common good, transformation, and self-interest) indicators are 41-26-33 for the employees in Company A and 38-26-36 for the employees in Company B. Both groups have the same proportion of values at the level of transformation but the people in Company A score slightly higher in the common good (C) (41%) than those in Company B (38%).

The comparison of current culture values (Figure 6–3) shows a high degree of alignment with eight matching values between the two cultures

[2] Normally we see two or three relationship values in the top ten personal values. Four or more relationship values indicates an above-average focus on people.

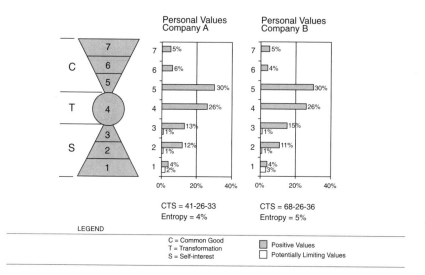

CTS = 41-26-33   CTS = 68-26-36
Entropy = 4%   Entropy = 5%

LEGEND

C = Common Good
T = Transformation   ▨ Positive Values
S = Self-interest   ☐ Potentially Limiting Values

Figure 6–2   Distribution of personal values of employees of Company
A and Company B

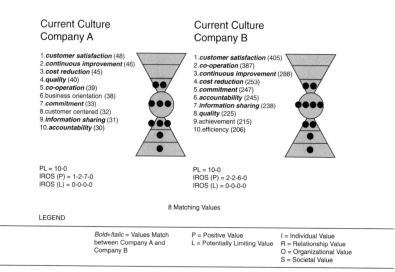

Current Culture
Company A

1. *customer satisfaction* (48)
2. *continuous improvement* (46)
3. *cost reduction* (45)
4. *quality* (40)
5. *co-operation* (39)
6. business orientation (38)
7. *commitment* (33)
8. customer centered (32)
9. *information sharing* (31)
10. *accountability* (30)

Current Culture
Company B

1. *customer satisfaction* (405)
2. *co-operation* (387)
3. *continuous improvement* (288)
4. *cost reduction* (253)
5. *commitment* (247)
6. *accountability* (245)
7. *information sharing* (238)
8. *quality* (225)
9. achievement (215)
10. efficiency (206)

PL = 10-0   PL = 10-0
IROS (P) = 1-2-7-0   IROS (P) = 2-2-6-0
IROS (L) = 0-0-0-0   IROS (L) = 0-0-0-0

8 Matching Values

LEGEND

Bold+Italic = Values Match   P = Positive Value   I = Individual Value
between Company A and   L = Potentially Limiting Value R = Relationship Value
Company B   O = Organizational Value
                                                                  S = Societal Value

Figure 6–3   Current culture values of Company A and Company B

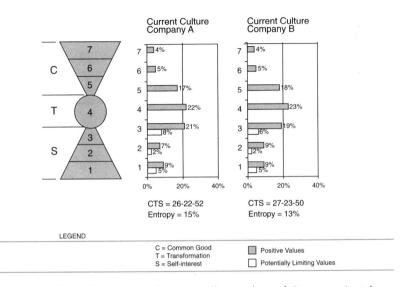

C = Common Good
T = Transformation
S = Self-interest

☐ Positive Values
☐ Potentially Limiting Values

Figure 6–4   Distribution of current culture values of Company A and Company B

and similar IROS distributions. The cultural entropy in Company A is 15%, and in Company B, it is 13% (Figure 6–4). Company B operates from a level of consciousness slightly higher than that of Company A. The CTS indicator for Company A is 26-22-52 and for Company B, it is 27-23-50.

The comparison of desired culture (Figure 6–5) values is also very similar with seven matching values between the two sets of values and similar IROS distributions. The distribution of desired cultural values in Company A is 35-26-39, and in Company B, it is 34-25-41 (Figure 6–6). The employees of Company A want to operate at a slightly higher level of consciousness than the employees of Company B. This is in alignment with both groups' personal values: Employees in Company A operate from a slightly higher level of consciousness than Company B. What is interesting is that the current culture of Company B already operates with a slightly higher level of consciousness than Company A. In other

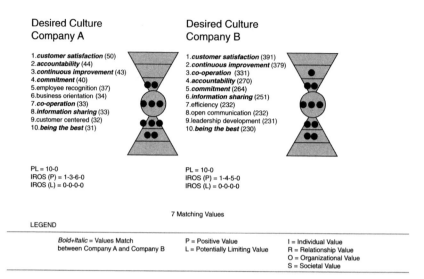

Desired Culture
Company A

1.*customer satisfaction* (50)
2.*accountability* (44)
3.*continuous improvement* (43)
4.*commitment* (40)
5.employee recognition (37)
6.business orientation (34)
7.*co-operation* (33)
8.*information sharing* (33)
9.customer centered (32)
10.*being the best* (31)

PL = 10-0
IROS (P) = 1-3-6-0
IROS (L) = 0-0-0-0

Desired Culture
Company B

1.*customer satisfaction* (391)
2.*continuous improvement* (379)
3.*co-operation* (331)
4.*accountability* (270)
5.*commitment* (264)
6.*information sharing* (251)
7.efficiency (232)
8.open communication (232)
9.leadership development (231)
10.*being the best* (230)

PL = 10-0
IROS (P) = 1-4-5-0
IROS (L) = 0-0-0-0

7 Matching Values

LEGEND

Bold+Italic = Values Match between Company A and Company B	P = Positive Value L = Potentially Limiting Value	I = Individual Value R = Relationship Value O = Organizational Value S = Societal Value

Figure 6–5   Desired culture values of Company A and Company B

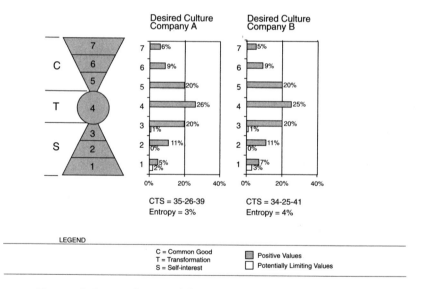

Desired Culture
Company A

7 6%
6 9%
5 20%
4 26%
3 1% 20%
2 0% 11%
1 5% 2%

0%   20%   40%

CTS = 35-26-39
Entropy = 3%

Desired Culture
Company B

7 5%
6 9%
5 20%
4 25%
3 1% 20%
2 0% 11%
1 7% 3%

0%   20%   40%

CTS = 34-25-41
Entropy = 4%

LEGEND

C = Common Good T = Transformation S = Self-interest	▓ Positive Values ☐ Potentially Limiting Values

Figure 6–6   Distribution of desired culture values of Company A
and Company B

words, Company B is better placed to provide what the employees of Company A want.

What we see in this example are two companies that will have very few difficulties in merging from a cultural perspective. The differences that exist are small, and they tend to enhance the merger rather than undermine it.

Merger 2: Department A and Department B

This is a merger of two university departments where Department A is being integrated into Department B. Comparisons of personal, current culture, and desired culture values of Departments A and B are shown in Figures 6–7 to 6–12.

The comparison of personal values shows four matching values with a 70% alignment in terms of levels of consciousness (Figure 6–7). Both groups share the same top two values—honesty and humor/fun. The

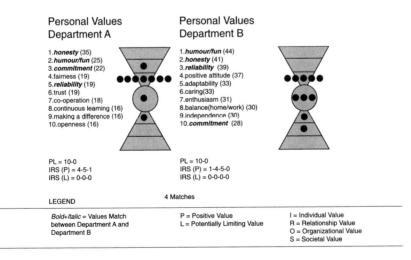

Figure 6–7 Personal values of employees in Departments A and B

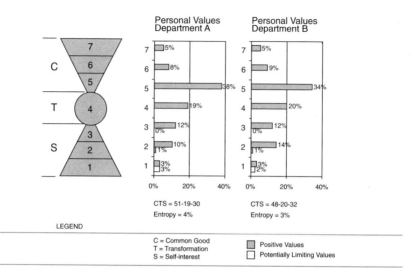

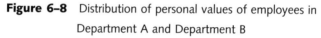

Figure 6–8   Distribution of personal values of employees in
Department A and Department B

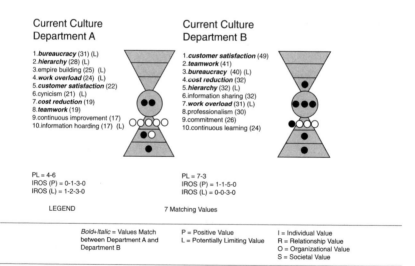

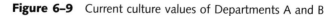

Figure 6–9   Current culture values of Departments A and B

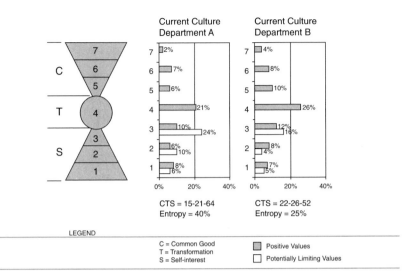

LEGEND

Figure 6–10   Distribution of current culture values of Departments
A and B

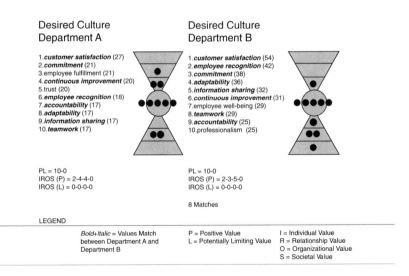

Figure 6–11   Desired culture values of Departments A and B

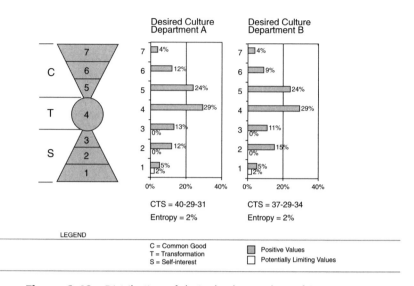

Figure 6–12   Distribution of desired culture values of Departments
A and B

people in Department A are highly people-oriented, with an IRS of 4-5-1. The distribution of personal values for the people in the two departments is very similar. The CTS index for the people in Department A is 51-19-30, and the CTS index for the people in Department B is 48-20-32. The people in Department A operate from a slightly higher consciousness than those in Department B (Figure 6–8).

The comparison of current culture values shows that the two groups share six matching values. Three of these are positive—customer satisfaction, teamwork, and cost reduction—and three are potentially limiting—bureaucracy, hierarchy, and work overload. There is an 80% alignment in terms of levels of consciousness (Figure 6–9). The culture of Department A is significantly more toxic (six potentially limiting values) than Department B with three potentially limiting values. The level of cultural entropy in Department A is 40%, and in Department B, it is 25% (Figure 6–10).

The comparison of desired culture values shows that the two groups share eight matching values. The IROS indicators for both groups are also compatible. If employee fulfillment can be regarded as being similar to employee well-being, the two departments share nine matching desired culture values. There is an 80% alignment in terms of levels of consciousness (Figure 6–11). The CTS indices for the desired culture values are very similar: Department A is 40-29-31 and Department B is 37-29-34. Basically, the employees in both departments want the same type of culture.

This realization and the fact that the cultures of both departments were not meeting employees' needs helped the leadership teams recognize the importance of seizing the opportunity to create a new culture out of the merger. They decided to make cultural transformation an integral part of the process of merging the two departments.

It is interesting to note that the two departments can support each other in some key areas. One of the issues in Department A is information hoarding; one of the things that Department B is good at is information sharing. Department A is looking for more commitment; Department B has commitment in their current culture.

The Values of the Leadership Group

Some of you may have noticed an apparent small anomaly in the data of Merger 1—Company A and Company B. You may be asking, "How could a group of people with a lower personal consciousness (Company B) create a slightly higher consciousness organization than a group of people with a slightly higher personal consciousness (Company A)?" The answer is that "They did not." The leadership group created the culture. When we separated out the data for the leadership group of Company B, we found that it operates at a higher level of consciousness than the rest of the employees, and at a slightly higher level of consciousness than the leadership group of Company A.

We have found that the link between the level of consciousness of the leadership group and the level of consciousness of the organization is a significant factor in diagnosing the cultural issues of an organization. Based on the hundreds of surveys we have carried out, we have been able to develop some relatively hard and fast rules about organizational cultures and leadership groups.

> Rule 1: An organization cannot operate at a higher level of consciousness than the personal consciousness of the leadership group.
>
> Rule 2: The culture of an organization is either a reflection of the personal consciousness of the leadership group (conscious and subconscious) or is inherited from previous leadership groups.
>
> Rule 3: In general, most organizations operate with a "default" culture because it arises unconsciously; the culture is not managed, the culture is not monitored, and the culture is simply recognized as "the way things are done around here."

In such situations, when the leadership group first sees the results of the cultural values assessment, they are shocked to find that the culture they administer is lower than their personal consciousness. They have fallen into the trap of accepting "this is the way things are done around here." They are not conscious of what they have created and they are unskilled at creating the culture they want to experience. They do not realize that by changing their collective behaviors they can change the culture.

Getting involved in a whole-system cultural transformation exercise enables the leadership group to become consciously skilled at creating the culture they want to experience as they get feedback from their colleagues (see Chapter 7) and participate in personal alignment and group-cohesion workshops (see Chapter 9). The introduction of a values-management process (see Chapter 11) to regularly measure their individual and collective behaviors enables them to create a high-performance, values-driven organization that seeks to enhance its cultural capital by becoming a full-spectrum consciousness organization.

Our research has shown that the cultures created by leadership groups can be categorized into five basic types characterized by the distribution of cultural entropy across different hierarchical levels of the organization.

Shadow Culture

The shadow culture is typified by a high level of cultural entropy in the leadership group that gradually decreases as you move down the hierarchical levels (Figure 6–13). The dysfunction of the personalities of the leadership group casts a shadow across the organization. The further away from the leadership group you get, the less impact the shadow has on the work culture.

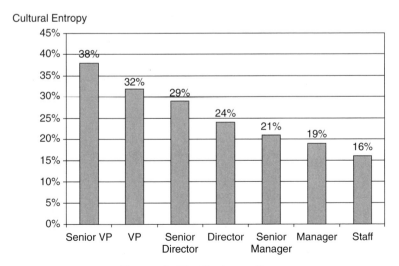

Figure 6–13 Shadow culture

Cultural Entropy

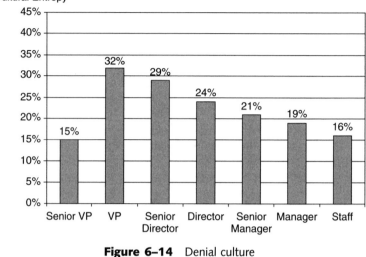

Figure 6–14   Denial culture

Denial Culture

The denial culture is typified by a low level of cultural entropy in the leadership group that rises sharply at the next level and then decreases gradually toward the lower echelons of the hierarchy (Figure 6–14). The leadership group lives in their own world unaware or impervious to the chaos they have created around them. They live in denial of the culture they have created. The direct reports of the leadership group have to deal with the dysfunction caused by their bosses.

Squeeze Culture

The squeeze culture is typified by a low or medium level of cultural entropy in the leadership group that gradually increases towards the middle management levels and then gradually decreases towards the

Cultural Entropy

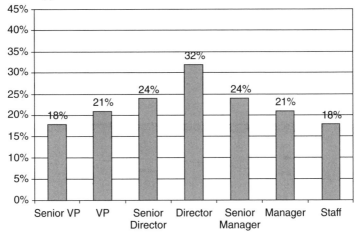

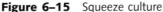

Figure 6–15   Squeeze culture

lower echelons of the hierarchy (Figure 6–15). The dysfunction occurs at the middle-management levels, not because of dysfunction from above as in the denial culture, but because of the delegated accountability for producing results being pushed down to the managerial level. The middle managers come under intense pressure from above to produce results and from below to make decisions. This type of culture arises when managers are given accountability without authority.

Crisis Culture

The crisis culture is typified by a pervasive high level of cultural entropy throughout all levels of the organization (Figure 6–16). This type of culture is often found in the public sector, where there are strong bureaucratic tendencies and rigid hierarchies. Part of the problem is that the leaders feel powerless to change the culture because of political

Cultural Entropy

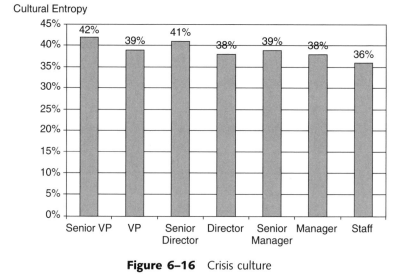

Figure 6–16   Crisis culture

interference and/or strong unionization. Our experience suggests that both the political masters and the union bosses will willingly collaborate when they understand the purpose of cultural transformation and can appreciate the change in climate and performance that will flow from a culture-change project. Both groups need to be brought on board at an early stage in the process by sharing with them the compelling reasons for change (see Chapter 9).

Values-Driven Culture

The values-driven culture is typified by a low level of cultural entropy throughout all levels of the organization (Figure 6–17). Values-driven cultures are products of a values-management process and/or the result of inspired leadership and are the highest performing cultures. Values-

Cultural Entropy

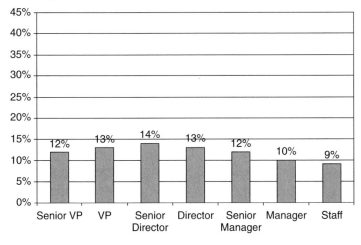

Figure 6–17   Values-driven culture

driven cultures are typically consciously created: The leader and the leadership team choose the values of the organization and actively live them. They reinforce the values by constantly referring to them and make them part of every organizational system and process. They sustain a high-performing culture by regularly mapping the culture and the individual performance of every executive and manager (see Chapter 11). Promotions are not based on performance results alone, but on the executive's or manager's ability to live the values.

Conclusions

We can classify the first four of these cultures as "default" cultures because they arise unconsciously. They are an expression of the personalities of the past and present leaders of the organization. No one has consciously attempted to manage the culture of the organization and there has been no attempt at values management. Conversely, the fifth type of culture is values-driven. In such cultures the leadership group consciously creates the culture they want to experience and actively manages their cultural capital.

7

Leadership: The Key to Cultural Transformation

My purpose in the previous chapters was to show how the cultural transformation tools (CTT) are used to provide a detailed diagnostic of an organizational culture and to introduce the concept of values management—a topic described in greater depth in Chapter 11. In this chapter and the next, we will explore two interrelated topics: leadership development and whole-system change. Let us begin with leadership development.

Here are some key facts about leadership and shareholder value.

Fact 1: Leadership development drives employee fulfillment.

Fact 2: Employee fulfillment drives customer satisfaction.

Fact 3: Customer satisfaction drives shareholder value.

Thus, as we see in Figure 7–1, there is a causal link between leadership development and shareholder value that passes through employee fulfillment and customer satisfaction. This link is present in all successful companies. This is in perfect alignment with the mantra outlined in *Liberating the Corporate Soul*:

> Organizational transformation begins with the personal transformation of the leaders. Organizations do not transform; people do!

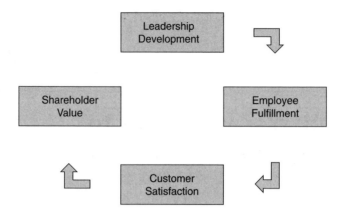

Figure 7–1 Leadership development to shareholder value

Here are some more facts:

Fact 4: Cultural alignment can occur at any level of consciousness, but only full-spectrum consciousness creates sustainable high performance and long-term resilience.

Fact 5: Achieving full-spectrum organizational consciousness requires full-spectrum leaders.

The challenge therefore in implementing cultural transformation projects is to change the behaviors of the leadership group and the senior level managers. They are responsible for creating the current culture, and they are the ones who must create the new culture. The chief executive officer (CEO) or the leader of the organization must be willing and committed to his or her own personal transformation to change the culture. The leaders must live the change they want to see in the culture of the organization. For each member of the leadership group, personal alignment to the organization's values and group cohesion around the vision, mission, values, and behaviors must become part of his or her personal journey.

Not everyone in the leadership group understands the need for this journey or is willing to participate. For those who are driven by achievement and operate from self-interest—the lower levels of consciousness—the prospect of such a journey is unimaginable at this point in their lives. They are wedded to their current way of being because it has been successful for them personally, and they cannot contemplate another way of acting. They will resist or try to undermine any form of change that requires a shift in behavior. They are stuck in the lower levels of consciousness where self-interest dominates the common good. They are left with two choices: Make the effort or get off the bus.

In Jim Collins' latest book, *From Good To Great*,[1] he states that the first job of a new leader is to get the right people in the right seats on the bus and that this is absolutely fundamental to building a long-lasting successful company. The right people are those who display what he refers to as level 5 leadership. In my terminology, Collins's level 5 leaders are those who display full-spectrum consciousness.

What are the characteristics of a full-spectrum leader? To answer this question, we need to understand the seven levels of leadership consciousness.

The Seven Levels of Leadership Consciousness

There are seven well-defined levels of leadership that correspond to the seven levels of organizational consciousness. Each level of leadership corresponds to the satisfaction of the needs of the organization at the corresponding level of consciousness. Leaders who learn to master the needs of every level of organizational consciousness operate from full-spectrum consciousness. Our research shows that these are

[1] Jim Collins. *Good to Great*. New York: HarperCollins, 2001.

Table 7–1   The Seven Levels of Leadership Consciousness

Level	Motivation	Leadership Focus
7	Service	Wisdom/Visionary: Service to humanity and the planet
6	Making a difference	Mentor/Partner: Strategic alliances and partnerships, mentoring, and coaching
5	Internal cohesion	Integrator/Inspirer: Developing a strong cohesive culture
4	Transformation	Facilitator/Influencer: Adaptability, continuous renewal, and learning
3	Self-esteem	Manager/Organizer: High-performance systems and processes
2	Relationship	Relationship Manager/Communicator: Relationships that support the organization
1	Survival	Crisis Director/Accountant: Pursuit of profit and shareholder value

the most resilient and successful leaders because they have the ability to respond appropriately to all internal challenges and external threats, while taking full advantage of opportunities for the organization to grow and develop. The seven levels of leadership consciousness are shown in Table 7–1.

The principle focus of the lower levels of leadership consciousness is on creating a financially stable organization with a strong customer base that has efficient systems and processes. The principle focus of the transformation level of leadership consciousness is to promote a climate of continuous learning and employee empowerment so that the organization can be responsive and adaptable to changes in its internal and external environment and continuously develop new products and services. The principle focus of upper levels of leadership consciousness is to create a vision, mission, and values for the organization that builds internal and external connectivity through strategic alliances and makes a contribution to society. The seven levels of leadership are described below in detail.

Level 1: The Crisis Director/Accountant

Level 1 leaders understand the importance of profit and shareholder returns. They manage their budgets meticulously. They look after the health and safety of employees. They are appropriately cautious in complex situations. They are effective in dealing with short-term issues and goals. One of the most important attributes of level 1 leaders is the ability to handle crises. When the survival of the organization is threatened, they know how to take control. They are calm in the midst of chaos and decisive in the midst of danger. Dealing with difficult, urgent situations often forces leaders to behave like authoritarians. However, when leaders operate as authoritarians on a regular basis, they quickly lose the trust and commitment of their people. Often the reason leaders use a dictatorial style to get what they want is because they find it difficult to relate to people in an open and effective way. Authoritarians are not used to asking for things; they are more comfortable giving orders. They are afraid to let go the reins of power because they have difficulty in trusting others. The greater their existential fears, the more risk-averse they become. They are quick to anger and are unable to discuss emotions. If they have insecurities around money, they will exploit others for their own financial ends. They are greedy in the midst of plenty, and enough is never enough. Fear-driven authoritarians create unhealthy climates in which to work. They promote a culture of compliance, but go no further than they have to in satisfying legal regulations.

Level 2: The Relationship Manager/Communicator

Relationship managers handle conflicts easily and invest a lot of time in building harmonious working relationships. They do not run away or hide from their emotions. They use their relationship skills to handle difficult interpersonal issues and their communication skills to build loyalty with their employees. They deliver good news and bad news with equal ease. They believe in open communication. They acknowledge and praise staff for a job well done. They are accessible to their employees and generous with their time. They are actively involved with customers and give priority to customer satisfaction. However, when leaders have fears about being liked, or are afraid to deal with their own or others' emotions, they avoid conflicts, are less than truthful in their interpersonal communications, and resort to manipulation to get what they want. They protect themselves by blaming others when things go wrong. Relationship managers are often protective of their people, but can demand loyalty, discipline, and obedience in return. They readily embrace tradition and often operate as paternalists. Paternalists find it difficult to trust people who are not part of the "family." They are secretive and engage in "mafia" politics. This lack of trust in outsiders by paternalist leaders can severely limit the pool of talent that the organization can draw on. Because paternalists demand obedience, they tend to crush the entrepreneurial spirit of employees. Paternalism frequently shows up in family-run businesses.

Level 3: The Manager/Organizer

Managers bring logic and science to their work. They use metrics to manage performance. They build systems and processes that create order and efficiency and enhance productivity. They are logical and rational in making decisions and have strong analytical skills. Managers think strategically and move quickly to capitalize on opportunities. Inwardly focused managers are good at organizing information and monitoring results. Outwardly focused managers anticipate workflow problems and get things done. They plan and prioritize their work and provide stability and continuity; create schedules and enjoy being in control; focus on their careers and are willing to learn new skills if it will help them in their professional growth. They want to learn the latest management techniques so they can achieve quality and excellence. They want to be successful and they want to be the best. When managers' needs for self-esteem are driven by subconscious fears, they become hungry for power, authority or recognition, or all three. They build empires to display their power. They build bureaucracies and hierarchies to demonstrate their authority. They compete with their colleagues to gain recognition. Their need for self-esteem can lead them to work long hours and neglect their families. Image is important to them and they will play office politics to get what they want.

Level 4: The Facilitator/Influencer

Facilitators seek advice, build consensus, and empower their staff. They recognize that they do not have to have all the answers. They give people responsible freedom; thus, making them accountable for outcomes and results. They research and develop new ideas. They consistently evaluate risks before embarking on new ventures. They resist the temptation to micro-manage the work of their direct reports. They promote participation, equality and diversity. They ignore or remove hierarchy. They are adaptable and flexible. They embrace continuous learning. They actively engage in their own personal development and encourage their staff to participate in programs that promote personal growth. They are looking to find balance in their lives through personal alignment. Balance leads to detachment and independence, and allows them to become objective about their strengths and weaknesses. They are learning to release their fears so they can move from being outer-directed to being inner-directed. They are in the process of self-actualization. As they let go of the need for outer approval, they begin to discover who they really are. They become enablers of others, encouraging them to express themselves, and share their ideas. They encourage innovation, focus on team building, enjoy challenges, and are courageous and fearless in their approach to life. Facilitators are in the process of shifting from being a manager to becoming a leader.

Level 5: The Integrator/Inspirer

The integrator/inspirer builds a vision and mission for the organization that inspires employees and customers alike. They promote a shared set of values and demonstrate congruent behaviors that guide decision-making throughout the organization. They are living examples of values-based leadership. They build cohesion and focus by bringing values alignment and mission alignment to the whole company. In so doing, they enhance the company's capacity for collective action. By creating an environment of openness, fairness and transparency, they build trust and commitment among their people. The culture they create unleashes enthusiasm, passion, and creativity at all levels of the organization. They are more concerned about getting the best result for everyone rather than their own self-interest. They are focused on the common good. They walk their talk. They are creative problem solvers. They view problems from a systems perspective, seeing beyond the narrow boundaries of cause and effect. They are honest and truthful and display integrity in all they do. They feel confident in handling any situation. This confidence and openness allows them to reclassify problems as opportunities. They clarify priorities by referring to the vision and mission. They display emotional intelligence as well as intellectual intelligence. Integrator/Inspirers are good at bringing the best out of people.

Level 6: Mentor/Partner

Mentor/partners are motivated by the need to make a difference in the world. They are true servant leaders. They create mutually beneficial partnerships and strategic alliances with other individuals or groups who share the same goals. They collaborate with customers and suppliers to create win-win situations. They are active in the local community and building relationships that create goodwill. They recognize the importance of environmental stewardship, and will go beyond the needs of compliance in making their operations environmentally friendly. They display empathy. They care about their people and seek ways to help employees find personal fulfillment through their work. They create an environment where people can excel. They are active in building a pool of talent for the organization by mentoring and coaching their subordinates. They are intuitive decision-makers, inclusive, and on top of their game.

Level 7: Wisdom/Visionary

Wisdom/visionary leaders are motivated by the need to serve the world. Their vision is global. They are focused on the questions, "How can I help?" and "What can I do?" They are concerned about the state of the world. They also care about the legacy they are leaving for future generations. They are not prepared to compromise long-term outcomes for short-term gains. They use their influence to create a better world. They see their own mission and that of their organization from a larger, societal perspective. They are committed to social responsibility. For them, the world is a complex web of interconnectedness, and they know and understand their role. They act with humility and compassion. They are generous in spirit, patient, and forgiving by nature. They are at ease with uncertainty and can tolerate ambiguity. They enjoy solitude and can be reclusive and reflective. Level 7 leaders are admired for their wisdom and vision.

The values of managers and leaders are usually distributed across three or four adjacent levels of consciousness. Managers' values are clustered in the lower levels of consciousness; leaders' values are clustered in the higher levels of consciousness.

Full-Spectrum Consciousness

The most successful leaders are those who have learned how to master every level of consciousness.

- They master level 1 by taking care of financial stability and employee safety.
- They master level 2 by focusing on open communication, respect, and customer satisfaction.

- They master level 3 by focusing on performance, results, and best practices.
- They master level 4 by focusing on adaptability, innovation, employee empowerment, and continuous learning.
- They master level 5 by developing a cohesive culture based on a shared vision and shared values that build resilience and a strong capacity for collective action.
- They master level 6 by building strategic alliances with like-minded partners; providing mentoring and coaching for their managers and leaders; and embracing environmental stewardship.
- They master level 7 by embracing social responsibility, ethics, global thinking, and holding a long-term perspective on their business and its impact on future generations.

How Do Leaders Become Full-Spectrum?

The simple answer to this question is through education, experience, and training. But, these three modes of learning are not enough. Managers and leaders must get regular feedback from their colleagues if they are to grow and develop into full-spectrum leaders. The feedback must be given in such a way that it provides personal insights within a mentoring or coaching environment. The most important aspect of the feedback is the juxtaposition of the individual leader's perception of himself or herself against his or her colleagues' perception of them. This is without a doubt the fastest way to grow. We are often unaware of how we come across to other people. Others sometimes see what we consider to be our strengths as our weaknesses. To find out where you are on the Seven Levels of Leadership, a self-assessment questionnaire can be found at www.valuescentre.com/leaders/index.htm.

Mentoring

Mentoring the CEO can be vital during the implementation of a whole-system cultural transformation program. The idea behind mentoring is that the leader has someone to talk to on an ongoing basis that can help him or her grow and develop the organization. For the CEO, this "someone" is often a professional mentor—a highly experienced individual outside the organization who is remunerated for his or her services: someone who has been a CEO for a significant period of time who can support the CEO on his or her journey. The return on such an investment can be immeasurable. CEOs often take on a professional mentor for 6 to 12 months when they move to a new company or first take on the position of CEO. For other senior people, a mentor may be someone in the organization or a sister organization, who is at the same or a higher level. Another way of getting support is for the CEO to join a chief executive's club or association where CEOs meet regularly in small groups to discuss topics of mutual interest.

Values-Based Coaching

Coaching is different to mentoring in that it is focused on helping an *individual* grow and develop as a person, as opposed to helping an individual grow and develop the *organization*. Coaching plays a vital part in a cultural transformation program by supporting the leaders and senior executives in living the organization's values—we call this "walking the talk." If the leaders are unable to role model the values by living the associated behaviors, then the cultural transformation of the organization will not take place. As previously stated, organizational transformation begins with the personal transformation of the leaders. The best way, and perhaps the only sure way, to make this happen is through coaching the individuals in the executive team and their direct reports.

The instrument we use to coach executives is called the leadership values assessment (LVA). A variant of this instrument is the leadership values and behaviors assessment (LVBA). The LVBA is similar to the LVA but in addition to mapping the executive's operational values and getting feedback on them, the instrument allows the assessors to also provide feedback on the degree to which the executive is living the behaviors that support the values of the organization. The behavior assessment (BA), with or without coaching, can be used independently from the LVBA as a quarterly feedback assessment.

The LVA works in the following way. The executive goes online and selects ten values/behaviors from a customized list of 80+ words or phrases that best describes how he or she operates. They also describe, in their own words, what they believe are their strengths, what they believe they need to work on, and what they are doing to change. Meanwhile, 15 or more colleagues, specifically chosen by the executive, go online and pick ten values/behaviors, from the same customized list, that they believe best describe the leader's operating style. They also describe the leader's strengths, the areas that he or she needs to work on, and any other feedback they want the person to have. The results are plotted against the seven levels of leadership model and the executive's perception of the distribution of his or her values is compared to the assessors' perception. A report is prepared and the results are delivered in a 2-hour coaching session. At the end of the coaching session, the leader develops a personal development plan.

The LVA and LVBA are among the most powerful coaching tools we offer. Significant results are obtained in more than 95% of cases. Even the disbelievers who tell us "people cannot change" are impressed by the results obtained from this process. People can change, and do change, especially when they receive feedback in a supportive environment from people whom they respect and trust.

The following paragraphs provide some case histories of the use of the LVA instrument.

Leadership Values Assessments

Leader A

Figure 7–2 shows that Leader A is good with people, but does not yet operate from full-spectrum consciousness. There are six matching values between Leader A's perception of herself and the perceptions of her assessors. Furthermore, all the values chosen by the assessors, except one, correspond to the same levels of consciousness as the values chosen by leader. These are the marks of authenticity. Leader A is an authentic, self-actualized individual, who knows herself, and who brings the best out of

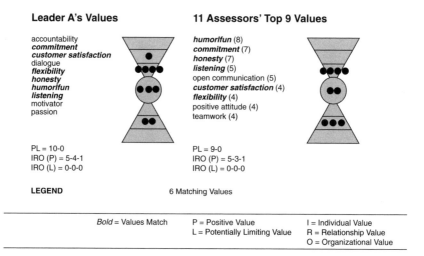

Leader A's Values	11 Assessors' Top 9 Values
accountability	*humor/fun* (8)
commitment	*commitment* (7)
customer satisfaction	*honesty* (7)
dialogue	*listening* (5)
flexibility	open communication (5)
honesty	*customer satisfaction* (4)
humor/fun	*flexibility* (4)
listening	positive attitude (4)
motivator	teamwork (4)
passion	

PL = 10-0   PL = 9-0
IRO (P) = 5-4-1   IRO (P) = 5-3-1
IRO (L) = 0-0-0   IRO (L) = 0-0-0

LEGEND   6 Matching Values

Bold = Values Match	P = Positive Value	I = Individual Value
	L = Potentially Limiting Value	R = Relationship Value
		O = Organizational Value

Figure 7–2   Leader A—leadership values assessment

her people. Leader A's strengths are her strong relationship skills, her focus on customer satisfaction, and her positive spirit. Leader A's areas of growth are in the financial arena (level 1) and in analytical matters (level 3). In addition to building skills around level 1 and level 3, Leader A needs to stretch herself to focus on employee fulfillment and/or become a mentor (level 6). She also needs to embrace issues such as ethics and social responsibility (level 7). These were the key areas of emphasis in her personal development plan. The coaching session focused on what Leader A could do to strengthen her level 1, 3, and 6 skills. Her profile suggests that she would be an excellent mentor.

Leader B

Figure 7–3 shows the results for Leader B who is anything but authentic. This is a passionate visionary who lacks emotional intelligence and creates havoc and chaos wherever he goes. He gives himself two positive

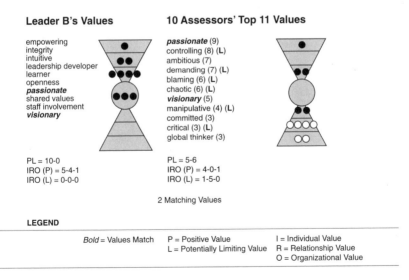

Leader B's Values

empowering
integrity
intuitive
leadership developer
learner
openness
passionate
shared values
staff involvement
visionary

PL = 10-0
IRO (P) = 5-4-1
IRO (L) = 0-0-0

10 Assessors' Top 11 Values

passionate (9)
controlling (8) (L)
ambitious (7)
demanding (7) (L)
blaming (6) (L)
chaotic (6) (L)
visionary (5)
manipulative (4) (L)
committed (3)
critical (3) (L)
global thinker (3)

PL = 5-6
IRO (P) = 4-0-1
IRO (L) = 1-5-0

2 Matching Values

LEGEND

Bold = Values Match   P = Positive Value   I = Individual Value
L = Potentially Limiting Value   R = Relationship Value
O = Organizational Value

Figure 7–3   Leader B—leadership values assessment

relationship values. His assessors give him five potentially limiting relationship values and one potentially limiting individual value. He is living in a false world. His perception of reality is very different from that of his assessors. There are only two matching values between him and his assessors. His strengths are his commitment to his work, his passion about his topic, his intelligence and his global vision. His areas for improvement are relationship skills and empathy. His profile reminds one of the intellectual professor who is totally wrapped up in his work and oblivious to the impact that he has on those who surround him. Leader B's personal performance plan gave emphasis to the development of his emotional intelligence skills. In providing coaching to Leader B, emphasis was first given to his positive attributes, his vision, his passion, his commitment, and his global thinking. We then turned the focus to why he thought his values of empowering, leadership developer, and openness were not getting across. Gradually, he began to get some insights into how he could become less critical and controlling and more organized. His personal development plan included listening, and learning how to seek feedback from his colleagues on a regular basis.

Leader C

Figure 7–4 shows the results for Leader C, a self-actualized individual who comes across to his colleagues as an almost full-spectrum leader. What is interesting about Leader C is that he has strong relationship skills but is unaware of them. He is unconsciously skilled at level 2. He is also unconsciously skilled at level 3. He and his assessors agree that his most significant blind spot is his lack of attention to financial matters (level 1). However, all is not lost in this area since his assessors chose results orientation as a value. His well-rounded profile shows that this is a leader with whom people like to work. In the coaching session, we first explored

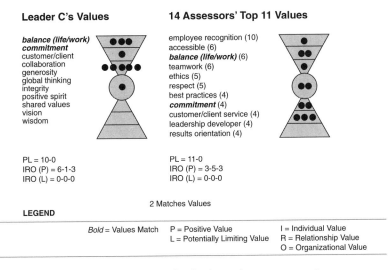

Leader C's Values

balance (life/work)
commitment
customer/client
collaboration
generosity
global thinking
integrity
positive spirit
shared values
vision
wisdom

PL = 10-0
IRO (P) = 6-1-3
IRO (L) = 0-0-0

14 Assessors' Top 11 Values

employee recognition (10)
accessible (6)
balance (life/work) (6)
teamwork (6)
ethics (5)
respect (5)
best practices (4)
commitment (4)
customer/client service (4)
leadership developer (4)
results orientation (4)

PL = 11-0
IRO (P) = 3-5-3
IRO (L) = 0-0-0

2 Matches Values

LEGEND

Bold = Values Match	P = Positive Value	I = Individual Value
	L = Potentially Limiting Value	R = Relationship Value
		O = Organizational Value

Figure 7–4   Leader C—leadership values assessment

his near full-spectrum leadership skills, bringing to his attention his mastery of level 2 and level 3. We then explored why so many of his values were not getting across to his colleagues. We confirmed with him that level 1 was a blind spot. Finally, we helped him create a personal development plan that involved giving more focus to financial matters and asking for regular feedback so he could become more aware of how he is perceived.

We always recommend that a leader shares the key points of his or her feedback and personal development plan with his or her colleagues, especially those who have provided feedback. We also suggest that leaders discuss their results with a spouse or significant other.

Several major companies have integrated our LVA and coaching process into their leadership development programs. These include major banks in Australia and Canada as well as a large number of mid-sized companies in Europe, South America, Europe, and the United States. One of the top ten companies to work for in the United States uses our LVA as part of their leadership development program.

Whole-System Change: The Context for Cultural Transformation

The Integral Model

As discussed in Chapter 1, the concept of whole-system change I am using in this book draws on four perspectives as shown in Figure 8–1.

- What is occurring in the consciousness of the individual is exemplified by the individual's *personality*—upper left quadrant.
- What is occurring in the consciousness of the collective is exemplified by the group *culture*—lower left quadrant.
- The outward manifestation of the consciousness of the individual in the form of personal actions and behaviors is exemplified by the individual's *character* —upper right quadrant; and
- The outward manifestation of the consciousness of the collective in the form of group actions and behaviors is exemplified by the collective's *social structures*—lower right quadrant.

The internal dimensions are the realms of the mind and its motivations—the values, beliefs, and thoughts that comprise the personality of

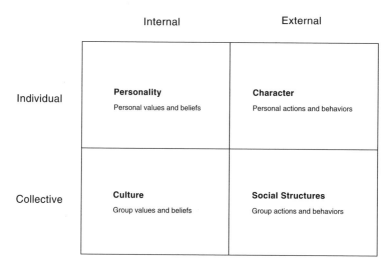

Internal   External

Individual

Personality
Personal values and beliefs

Character
Personal actions and behaviors

Collective

Culture
Group values and beliefs

Social Structures
Group actions and behaviors

Figure 8–1 Human systems—four quadrants

the individual and the values and beliefs that comprise the culture of the collective. This is the realm of consciousness. What is internal cannot be seen or observed; it can only be deduced by observing behaviors and entering into dialogue with people. These are the causal factors in all decision making in all human systems. The external dimensions are the realms of actions and behaviors. Actions and behaviors are driven by the conscious or subconscious motivations of an individual or a group, and their motivations are driven by their perceived needs.

Thus, all values and behaviors are related to needs, and all needs are related to specific levels of consciousness. What is external is the outward manifestation of the internal, which can be readily seen or observed.

When there is concordance between the stated values and beliefs of an individual or group and the actions and behaviors of the individual or group, there is authenticity and integrity. Where there is authenticity and integrity, there is a solid foundation for trust. The level of trust that exists in any human group structure, as Francis Fukuyama points out, is the single most pervasive characteristic for the creation of successful groups.[1]

We call this alignment between what we say and what we do "walking the talk" because as outside observers the only way we know what is going on internally in others is what they tell us. If the actions and behaviors of individuals or groups are in alignment with the values and beliefs that they tell us they espouse, then we consider this person or group to operate with authenticity or integrity. When the actions and behaviors of individuals or groups are not in concordance, there is a lack of authenticity and integrity and there is no foundation for trust.

For the purposes of explaining the concept of whole-system change, I propose the following definitions.

Personal alignment: The alignment of an individual's values and beliefs with his or her actions and behaviors—authenticity.

Structural alignment: The alignment of a group's values and beliefs with their actions and behaviors as codified in the collective rules, laws, and processes and structures of governance—integrity.

Values alignment: The alignment of an individual's values with the group's values.

Mission alignment: The alignment of an individual's sense of purpose or mission with the group's stated purpose or mission.

Values alignment and mission alignment together create group cohesion.

[1] Francis Fukuyama. *Trust: The Social Virtues and the Creation of Prosperity.* New York: Free Press, 1992.

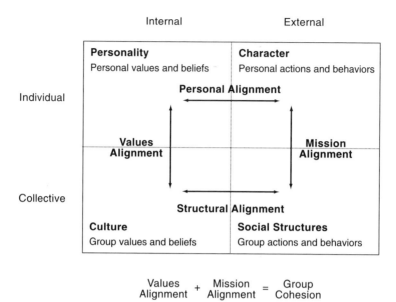

Figure 8–2 shows how these four types of alignment are superimposed on the four-quadrant matrix, where the internal dimensions are represented by values and beliefs and the external dimensions are represented by actions and behaviors.

For whole-system change to occur, there must be a parallel shift in personal alignment, structural alignment, values alignment, and mission alignment. All four relationships must change in the same direction for the group to experience a shift in consciousness. When all four relationships change in the same direction, the group finds a new level of internal stability and external equilibrium at a higher level of consciousness.

For example, when the results of a culture assessment show that an organization or group is operating from levels 1, 2, and 3 of consciousness, and the desired culture shows that they want to shift to level 4, there must be a parallel shift in the values, beliefs, actions, and behaviors of individuals, *and* in the values, beliefs, actions, and behaviors of the organization for this shift to occur. The shift to level 4 consciousness requires a recalibration of the individual and collective values and beliefs, particularly the values and beliefs of the leaders, and the values and beliefs of the group as they are expressed through the group's rules, regulations, and codes of conduct as well as the systems, processes, and procedures. In nations, we describe the shift to level 4 consciousness as democracy. In organizations, we describe the shift to level 4 consciousness as empowerment.

The way we bring about such a change in an organization is through workshops, seminars, and training programs that focus on personal alignment and group cohesion (values alignment and mission alignment), and structural alignment—changes to the rules, regulations, systems, processes, and structures of governance that reflect the values and behaviors of the new level of consciousness. Mistakes are often made in cultural transformation programs because these interdependencies are not well understood.

Common Mistakes

Mistake 1: Focus on Personal Alignment Only

Many organizations focus on personal alignment without doing anything about structural alignment. This serves only to aggravate the situation. Managers and employees who have experienced a personal alignment program shift to a higher level of personal consciousness while the rules, regulations, and systems and processes of the organization still reflect the old level of consciousness. This just serves to increase the overall level of frustration in the organization.

Mistake 2: Focus on Group Cohesion Only

Another frequent mistake is focusing on group cohesion (team building) without first carrying out a personal alignment program. This limits the potential for success of the group-cohesion program because people enter these programs without self-understanding or strong interpersonal skills. We want employees to come into a group-cohesion program having already experienced a shift in consciousness. Therefore, for maximum impact, personal alignment should precede group cohesion, and structural alignment should precede personal alignment or be implemented in parallel. When this happens organizations can shift smoothly to a new level of consciousness.

Mistake 3: Failure to Customize the Personal Alignment and Group-Cohesion Programs

The most frequent mistake is to use "off-the-shelf" personal alignment or group-cohesion programs. All personal alignment and group-cohesion programs need to be customized to the client situation for optimum results. "Cookie-cutter" personal alignment or team-building programs are potential recipes for failure.

The personal alignment and group-cohesion programs should be tailored to correspond to the levels of consciousness and world-views of the group. The seven levels of consciousness model (see Chapter 2) and spiral dynamics model (see Chapter 9) provide the necessary insights to design such programs. The cultural values assessment survey tells you exactly where the group is and where it wants to go in terms of values and levels of consciousness. The spiral dynamics assessment tells you where the group is with regard to its worldviews. These understandings are particularly important in choosing the implementation methodologies that are appropriate for the personal alignment and group-cohesion programs.

The group-cohesion program is built around a shared set of values and a shared vision and mission. If the leadership group has mastered level 4 consciousness, they will want to involve as many employees as possible in the definition of the vision, mission and values of the organization. If on the other hand the leadership group is operating from the lower three levels of consciousness, they will not want to involve the whole organization in this exercise. They will want to do the work themselves.

The process we use to identify the vision, mission and values in the former situation utilizes the techniques of appreciative inquiry.[2] The process we use to identify the vision, mission, and values in the latter situation is called the "four-whys process," and is described in detail in *Liberating the Corporate Soul: Building a Visionary Organization.*[3] An overview of the process is provided in the next chapter. This process also works well with individuals who are trying to discover a deeper meaning to their lives.

In both cases we use the cultural values assessment to garner employee's perceptions of the current and desired cultures. This process ensures that the leadership group has a clear understanding of the current strengths and weaknesses of the culture as they enter the visioning process.

---

[2] David L. Cooperrider, Peter F. Sorensen Jr., Diana Whitney, and Therese F. Yaeger, eds. *Appreciative Inquiry: Rethinking Human Organization Toward a Positive Theory of Change.* Champaign, IL: Stipes Publishing, 2000.

[3] Richard Barrett. *Liberating the Corporate Soul: Building a Visionary Organization* Boston: Butterworth-Heinemann, 1998; pp. 103–123.

Having identified the organization's vision and mission, the leadership group together with the employees must choose the values they want to live by. Simply identifying the values is not enough. Each value must be translated into three or four behavior statements. This is important because values are concepts that transcend contexts, whereas beliefs and behaviors are contextual. For example, the behaviors associated with the value of trust in a law firm will be different from the behaviors associated with the value of trust in a car factory. The values must be contextualized into behaviors before embarking on personal alignment, structural alignment, and group-cohesion programs. Contextualizing is important because it makes the values real and provides an objective measure of compliance. The behaviors associated with specific values can be used in monitoring the performance of individuals. For further discussion on values management see Chapter 11.

Table 8–1 provides three examples of values and their associated behaviors developed by a large Canadian organization. There are no off-the-shelf behaviors that one can ascribe to a particular value. What is important is that the behaviors speak to the needs of this particular group. The behaviors must be defined by the group in the context of their conditions of existence.

The point to stress here is that the personal alignment and the group-cohesion programs must not only be customized with language that reflects the belief structures and levels of consciousness of the group, they must also be designed to emphasize the chosen vision, mission, values, and behaviors. This is an opportunity to inculcate the vision, mission, values, and behaviors into the culture—an opportunity that should not be missed.

Personal alignment programs can be carried out with groups of 20 to 24 people from different parts of an organization because the focus is on self-knowledge, self-appreciation, and self-respect. They can also be carried out within intact teams. Group-cohesion programs, on the other

Table 8–1   Values and their Supporting Behaviors

Value	Supporting Behaviors
Accountability	Takes responsibility for his or her actions Admits mistakes, learns from them, and takes corrective action Does what he/she says and lives up to his/her commitments
Teamwork	Actively contributes and shares responsibility for results Respects the opinions of others and listens attentively Asks for input and feedback from team members
Trust	Is open and candid Treats others with dignity and fairness Operates with integrity and supports colleagues

hand, should always be carried out within intact teams. An intact team could be the senior executive group or the leaders of a business or functional unit.

One of the ways we link the process of personal alignment with group cohesion is to carry out 360-degree leadership values assessments (LVAs) and coaching sessions for the members of an intact team after they have experienced a personal alignment program and before they experience a group-cohesion program. In this way, they walk into the group-cohesion program with their personal development plan based on a clear understanding of the feedback they received from their subordinates, managers, and peers, some of whom will be part of the group-cohesion workshop. Sometimes, we carry out the LVA coaching sessions before the personal alignment program to build awareness for the need of a personal alignment program.

The group-cohesion program includes time for each member of the intact team to share the results of his or her personal development plan. The purpose of this sharing is to make personal transformation mutually accountable. When you and your colleagues stand in front of your teammates and commit to personal change, you are collectively making yourselves accountable to each other for a change in behavior. The group-cohesion program also includes a review of the team's and/or business unit's cultural values assessment.

The objective of the personal alignment, group cohesion (values and mission alignment), and structural alignment programs is to build group resilience. There are three aspects to group resilience:

(1) Cultural resilience
(2) Structural resilience
(3) Operational resilience

Cultural resilience involves heightening the group's capacity for communication, cooperation, coordination, collaboration, and building trust. Structural resilience involves building the organization's decision-making and governance structures so that accountability is clearly delineated. Operational resilience involves developing plans for disaster recovery and mitigation so that key business processes can be maintained under all operating conditions—mission assurance.

When there is a shock to the human system (individual or collective), disharmony and dysfunction will show up at the levels of consciousness that are the least developed or the least in alignment. These are also the levels of the least resilience. Only full-spectrum individuals and full-spectrum groups—those who are fearless and who have mastered the needs of every level of consciousness—are able to weather continuous shocks and achieve long-term sustainability.

Cultural Entropy

Cultural entropy, which is the proportion of energy in an organization consumed by nonproductive activities, occurs when there is a lack of alignment between the four quadrants. Cultural entropy is inversely related to resilience. When cultural entropy is high, resilience is low. When cultural entropy is low, resilience is high. There are four causes of cultural entropy.

Lack of Personal Alignment

Lack of personal alignment occurs when there is a lack of alignment between the stated values of individuals and their behaviors, particularly among the leadership group. When leaders are unable to walk the talk—when they display a lack of personal integrity—they are unable to build trust among each other and between themselves and their staff.

Lack of Structural Alignment

Lack of structural alignment occurs when there is a lack of alignment between the stated values of the group and the behaviors of the group as reflected in the rules, regulations, structures, and systems of governance. When the group does not live by its stated values, there is a loss of collective integrity. For example, when an organization embraces fairness and diversity, it must ensure that the processes used for employee promotions reflect these values. Without this alignment cynicism quickly breeds and employees will learn not to trust the systems and structures that support the culture.

Lack of Values Alignment

Lack of values alignment occurs when there is (a) a lack of alignment between the personal values of individuals and the collective values of the group and (b) a lack of alignment between the values expressed in the current culture and the desired culture. People are unable to bring their full selves to work and when they get to work, they are constantly fighting or frustrated by the culture. This leads to a lack of coherence, exemplified by fragmentation, separation, and empire building. In such situations self-interest takes precedence over the common good.

Lack of Mission Alignment

Lack of mission alignment occurs when there is a lack of alignment between the sense of purpose or mission of employees or their prime motivational drivers and the collective sense of purpose and mission of the group. This leads to a lack of focus, a lack of clarity, and a lack of engagement. When the objectives of the organization do not align with the objectives of individuals, the employees' energies cannot be channeled in the same direction. When there is coherence (values alignment), focus and clarity (mission alignment), and trust (personal alignment and structural alignment) there is a strong sense of group cohesion engagement, and an enhanced capacity for collective action.

Thus, we see that cultural entropy arises when there is a lack of coherence, lack of focus, lack clarity and lack of trust. All these conditions lead to a lowering of resilience and a decrease in the group's capacity for collective action.

The CTT cultural values assessment instrument clearly indicates at what levels of consciousness cultural entropy is occurring and at what levels of consciousness there is little or no resilience. In the case of Flexite, described in Chapter 4 the overall level of entropy is 28%, of which 10% is at level 1, 7% at level 2, and 11% at level 3 (see Figure 4–2). There is also a gap between the current culture and desired culture at levels 4, 5, 6, and 7. There is low resilience at all levels. This is a sick company with full-spectrum dysfunction. Many of the answers to the problems of Flexite can be found in the values chosen for the desired culture. The only way to turn this particular company around is to implement a whole-systems approach to cultural transformation.

9

The Framework for Whole-System Change

The framework for whole-system change can be divided into two phases:

Phase 1: Preparation, and
Phase 2: Implementation.

The preparation phase (Figure 9–1) culminates in the definition of a strategy for the implementation of a whole-system change program and the identification of the objectives and key performance indicators that will be used to measure the success of the program.

Preparation Phase

Step 1(a): Cultural Transformation Tools Values Assessment

The first step in the whole-system change preparation phase is to carry out a company-wide values assessment to identify employees' personal values, their perception of the current culture values, and their desired culture values. This is known as the baseline assessment. The procedure

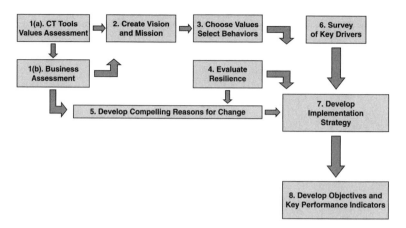

Figure 9–1   Whole-system change—preparation phase

for carrying out a baseline assessment and the outputs obtained are described in Chapter 4. The process should begin by mapping the values of the leadership group and their direct reports, and getting the commitment of the leadership group to behavioral change. The rest of the company is then surveyed. The values survey should include demographics such as position, business unit, location, and if appropriate gender, age, ethnicity, length of service, and so forth. The cultural values assessment will identify opportunities and obstacles to cultural change and provide guidance in the development of personal alignment, group cohesion, and structural alignment programs. It will also provide assistance in identifying the key performance indicators that will be used for values-management. For example, an organization that suffers from poor internal relationships might focus on building trust; an organization that is having difficulty producing ideas for new products or services might focus on encouraging creativity. In these cases "trust" and "creativity" would become key performance indicators in the process of values-management (see Chapter 11).

Step 1(b): Business Assessment

In developing the compelling reasons for change (step 5), it will be important to include the business case for change as well as the cultural case for change. The two, of course, are intimately linked. Usually, the business case for change is blatantly obvious from the financial results of the organization or key performance indicators such as employee retention, market share and customer satisfaction. What is important in making the case for cultural change is to draw the link between outcome measures such as profitability and causal measures such as cultural alignment or cultural entropy. The cultural values assessment will help to make this link. It not only identifies the "causal" reasons why earnings or productivity are low, why people find it difficult to be creative, and why performance is under par, it also provides quantitative measures related to these causes. One of the ways to build the business case for change is to benchmark the organization against a well-established business model such as the European Foundation for Quality Management excellence model (EFQM) or the U.S. Baldrige criteria. Chapter 14 provides an example of such an approach where the EFQM and the CTT have been integrated to develop a combined business and culture diagnostic.

Step 2: Create Vision and Mission

The purpose of this step is to give direction to the change process. We frequently find that organizations either pay no attention to their vision or mission statements or simply do not have them. If the organization does not have a vision and mission, this is an opportunity to create one. If the organization does have a vision and mission, this is an opportunity to revisit it. Often the vision and mission were created years earlier by a completely different team operating under different market conditions. The purpose of revisiting the vision and mission is to make sure it is still relevant and inspiring to the leadership group, the executive population, managers and staff. The process we normally use for revisiting the vision and mission or designing a new one for an organization is the four-whys process. This process is described in detail in *Liberating the Corporate Soul*.[1] If the leadership team is willing to involve the whole organization in this process, appreciative inquiry can be used for this purpose.

The four-whys process begins with the leadership group. There are three basic inputs to the process: (1) the results of the cultural values assessment; (2) the core motivations of the leadership group; and (3) the definition of the core business. The results of the cultural values assessment provide input from the employee population about what is and is not working in the current culture and what values they consider to be important. The core motivations of the leadership group are developed through a simple process of finding out each member's deepest motivation for coming to work, and then finding out what motivations the group has in common. The definition of the core business is arrived at by simply asking all members of the leadership group to write down what they believe is the core business of the group. The results are often fragmented and not sufficiently focused to give the group a clear intention. Agreement on the core business is essential before moving on. One of the ways to get at the core business is define the organization's principle economic engine—what is it that the organization does that is the main wealth/profit creating activity? Once the core business is clarified, the core motivations are known, and the most

[1] Richard Barrett. *Liberating the Corporate Soul: Building a Visionary Organization*. Boston: Butterworth-Heinemann, 1998; pp. 112–123.

important current and desired culture values are identified, it is relatively simple to build an inspiring vision and mission using the four-whys process.

The uniqueness of the four-whys process is that it defines an internal vision and mission and an external vision and mission. It separates the organization's purpose from its character—what it does in the world, from its way of being. The internal mission describes how the organization is going to grow and develop internally. The internal vision describes what the organization will look like in 5 to 10 years. The external mission describes what the organization does for its customers. The external vision describes the impact that the organization wants to have on society.

The vision and mission statements should be concise, inclusive, and easily memorized. They should reflect the interest of all stakeholders—employees, customers, the local community or nation, and shareholders.

The vision statement(s) declare the organization's intention with regard to the future it wants to create: It describes the "end" or what the "destination" looks like. The mission statement(s) on the other hand describe the "means" to the end—what the organization needs to focus on to get to the destination. The vision statement(s) can be characterized as, "This is where we are going," and the mission statement(s) can be characterized as, "This is what is absolutely essential for us to concentrate on in order to achieve our vision."

Ultimately, the real purpose of the vision and mission is to galvanize the intentions of each individual in the organization around the same purpose. Leaders, managers, and employees should have a clear line of sight between their sense of personal mission and the overall vision of the company. Every employee should know how he or she makes a difference to the bottom line of the organization and/or its mission assurance—its ability to deliver its primary services. This alignment of purpose generates a strong sense of commitment. Work becomes

Table 9–1 Examples of Vision and Mission Statements

Type of Company	External Vision	Internal Vision	Mission Statements
Bank	To be a leader in client relationships	Create an environment where all employees can excel	Help customers achieve what matters to them Make a real difference in the communities where we work Bring shareholders the highest total return on their investment
Business consulting firm	To change the philosophy of business at a global level	Be a global resource for organizational transformation	Support leaders in building values-driven organizations Build a worldwide network of consultants committed to organizational transformation

meaningful, and employees look forward to getting to work. People do not begrudge going the extra mile if their hearts and souls are aligned with what they do and the culture supports them in fulfilling their purpose. Table 9–1 provides some examples of vision and mission statements. More examples can be found in *Liberating the Corporate Soul*.[2]

Ultimately, the vision, mission, and values are guides to decision making. They are constant reminders, for the organization and for each individual, about the outcomes the organization wants to manifest. They are future-oriented. By keeping the vision, mission, and values constantly

[2] Richard Barrett. *Liberating the Corporate Soul: Building a Visionary Organization*. Boston: Butterworth-Heinemann, 1998; p. 111.

in focus, the organization creates a decision-making framework that is self-fulfilling. The organization consciously creates the future it wants to experience. As Collins and Porras point out in *Built to Last: Successful Habits of Visionary Companies*[3] the distinguishing feature of long-lasting successful companies is that they use their vision, mission, and values to guide decision making.

This is not how most organizations operate. They either do not have a vision and mission or if they do, they are not used to guide decision making. They are simply platitudes that are referred to when convenient or things to do that once done can be ticked off and forgotten as the organization moves its attention to the next task.

Step 3: Choose Values and Select Behaviors

The values of an organization serve three purposes—they provide guidelines for acceptable and unacceptable behaviors, they support the organization in creating the future it wants to experience, and they provide direction in decision making.

One of our clients has developed two categories of values—cornerstone values and operational values. The cornerstone values are the values that they regard as vital for the business to be successful. For example, an oil company might have profit, employee safety, and environmental awareness as cornerstone values. These are nonnegotiable values that they regard as fundamental for the successful running of their business. Cornerstone values can also be described as the principles or ideals. Sometimes they are expressed in the form of a credo. Operational values, on the other hand, are values that emphasize how people work

---

[3] James C. Collins and Jerry I. Porras. *Built to Last: Successful Habits of Visionary Companies.* New York: HarperBusiness, 1994.

together (trust, openness, fairness) and what is important on a day-to-day basis (cost reduction, quality, and productivity).

The process of choosing values should not be rushed. The values will become the "guidelines" or "rules" for decision making in the organization. Values that are shared build trust and create community. They create cohesion and a sense of unity. The results of the cultural values assessment provide significant insights as to what values leaders, managers, and employees consider important. For organizations operating from the lower levels of consciousness (levels 1, 2, and 3), the chosen values should stretch them to levels 4 and 5. Thus, for example in the case of Flexite, accountability (the number 3 desired cultural value) and teamwork (the number 12 desired cultural value) are both level 4 values and would make good choices for operational values. Innovation might also be a good choice. This is a level 4 value. At level 5, they might consider cooperation and trust (see Figure 4–1). The organization should choose no more than 3 or 4 values.

In *Value Shift*,[4] Lynn Sharp Paine, the John G. McLean Professor at the Harvard Business School, states that a chief executive officer's (CEO) reasons for embracing values tend to cluster in four main areas:

- Reasons relating to risk management
- Reasons relating to organizational functioning
- Reasons relating to market positioning
- Reasons relating to civic positioning.

She states that a fifth theme is that CEOs simply believe that it is the right thing to do. They believe that there is inherent worth in the values they are seeking to encourage. We have found from carrying out hun-

---

[4] Lynn Sharp Paine. *Value Shift*. New York: McGraw-Hill, 2003; p. 7.

dreds of cultural values assessments that this is true. This intuitive response is backed up by solid evidence that shows living your values builds bottom-line success. Lynn Sharp Paine sets out a new value proposition that convincingly links high ethical standards with outstanding financial results.[5]

The next step is to identify the behaviors that support the chosen values. Once again, the cultural values assessment helps craft these statements. For example, if trust were to be chosen as one of Flexite's values, the behavior statements should include open communication, cooperation, and commitment—all desired culture values.

> Trust is open and candid in all relationships
> Cooperates with colleagues to achieve common goals
> Inspires commitment through living the values

If "innovation" is chosen as a value for Flexite, then the behavior statements might mention values such as "continuous improvement" (the number 2 desired cultural value) and "teamwork" (the number 12 desired cultural value).

> Innovation
> Introduces new ideas that support continuous improvement
> Empowers team members to bring forth their ideas
> Encourages creative teamwork for improving performance

The behavior statements are written in such a way that they can be easily used in some form of performance monitoring process. They can also be used in the leadership values and behaviors assessment (LVBA). The feedback from this assessment provides a measure of the

---

[5] Ibid. pp. 133–165.

compliance of the leaders to both the espoused values and their associated behaviors.

Once the values have been chosen, the technology we use to identify
the behaviors associated with the values is known as appreciative inquiry.
This process is described in detail in Chapter 12.

Step 4: Evaluate Organizational Resilience

Before completing the preparation phase it is important to examine the
long-term sustainability of the organization by carrying out a baseline
evaluation of the organization's resilience. The objective is to find ways
to enhance the organization's ability to withstand shocks and anticipate
risks—find ways to build its adaptive capacity.

In *Corporate Culture and Performance*[6] Harvard Business School
researchers Kotter and Heskett stress the importance of adaptive
cultures.

> An adaptive culture entails risk-taking, trusting, and a proactive approach
> to organizational and individual life. Members actively support one
> another's efforts to identify all problems and implement workable solu-
> tions. There is a shared feeling of confidence: the members believe,
> without a doubt, that they can effectively manage whatever new problems
> or opportunities will come their way. There is widespread enthusiasm, a
> spirit of doing whatever it takes to achieve organizational success. The
> members are receptive to change and innovation.[7]

[6] John P. Kotter and James L. Heskett. *Corporate Culture and Performance.*
New York: The Free Press, 1992.

[7] John P. Kotter and James L. Heskett. *Corporate Culture and Performance.*
New York: The Free Press, 1992; pp. 44–45.

The focus of steps 1 through 3 in the whole-system change framework is to identify the parameters that will support the building of enterprise-wide cultural resilience. The focus of step 4 is to identify the parameters that support the building of enterprise-wide structural and operational resilience. To this end, the baseline resilience assessment should include a whole-system mapping of the organization's operational footprint, including critical network alliances, core business value chains, key business processes, strategic operational nodes, critical operational nodes, important assets, historical threats, and current high-impact risk issues associated with key business areas. The objective is to assess the organization's core capabilities with regard to managing both historical risk patterns and current low probability, high-impact risks that may not yet be on the organization's radar screen (see Chapter 13 for more information on building organizational resilience).

Step 5: Develop Compelling Reasons for Change

It is important before starting a process of whole-system change involving cultural transformation that the chief executive and the board have compelling reasons for change. There must be a clear understanding among the executive population, managers, and staff why the organization is embarking on a whole-system change process. The establishment of the compelling reasons for change begins at step 1 and is not completed until the end of step 4. It is a process of ongoing discovery as the organization takes a hard look at itself in the mirror.

For unsuccessful companies who are suffering from low performance, the compelling reasons for change are usually obvious. The cultural issues that underlie the poor performance can easily be identified from the results of the cultural values assessment. A convincing link must be made between the performance issues and the cultural issues. Usually, this is not difficult to do. The CEO and the leadership team should present a clarifying story so the reasons for the whole-system change effort are clearly understood and the support of the executive and employee populations can be enlisted. For successful companies, the compelling reasons for change are not usually about improving current performance; they are more about how they can position themselves to take advantage of future opportunities and build long-term resilience and sustainability.

The results of an organization-wide cultural values assessment provide significant inputs for the storyline of the compelling reasons for change, particularly when the cultural entropy of the organization is over 20%. Ultimately, the compelling reasons for change must be so convincing that they unite everyone behind the whole-system change process. The change process must be grounded in reality and driven by realistic optimism that provides the employee and executive populations with a hope for a better future.

The Cost of Fear

One technique we have developed to support the storyline of the "compelling reasons for change" is to calculate the "cost of fear" in an organization. Fear, both subconscious and conscious, is the motivating force behind many of the potentially limiting values that show up in a cultural values assessment. For example, internal competition is rooted in fears concerning self-esteem. We compete rather than collaborate because we are more focused on self-interest than the common good. People who practice internal competition see life as a zero-sum game with winners and losers. They must win at all costs. Empire building and information hoarding are motivated by similar needs. Hierarchy is rooted in fears concerning status and trust. Bureaucracy is rooted in fears concerning order and control.

The underlying fear in most hierarchical structures is "people cannot be trusted." Therefore, the argument goes, they must be supervised closely by people who are loyal to the system and can be trusted. The more loyal and trusted you are the more status you gain in the hierarchy. Those who seek self-esteem through status want to look good in the eyes of their superiors, so they are concerned about their image. They will blame others when things go wrong, and they will manipulate the system to finish up on top.

The underlying fears in bureaucracy are "things will fall apart if order is not maintained" and "people will cheat the system if there are no controls." Therefore, all transactions must be checked and double-checked. Bureaucracy and hierarchy feed off each other by giving people power over others. Power seeking leads to empire building—another fear-driven approach to achieving self-esteem consciousness.

All these activities that are based in fear create cultural entropy. The energy involved in "doing" internal competition, bureaucracy, hierarchy, empire building, image, blame, and information hoarding is not available for useful work. The effort and time that go into supporting these potentially limiting values result in a loss in productivity, efficiency, commitment, and opportunities. This is the basis for the "cost of fear" calculation.

After the cultural values assessment is completed, and the potentially limiting values are identified, we ask groups of employees at different levels of the organization to estimate the percentage impact of each of the potentially limiting values on lost productivity and lost opportunity. We aggregate the results by staff level and then multiply the average percentage impacts of each potentially limiting value on lost productivity by the total employee costs (salary plus benefits). We multiply the average percentage of lost opportunity by total sales. We add the results of these two calculations together to find out the financial impact of the cultural entropy on the organization.

We would be the first to admit that the results are not scientific. They do however provide an estimate of the monetary impact of the potentially limiting values on human performance. We have found that reducing the level of cultural entropy by 10 points—say from 30% to 20%—has a significant positive impact on the bottom line results. By creating a direct link between the level of cultural entropy and bottom line results, we can develop a story to support the process of cultural change that convinces even the most hard-nosed business types.

Step 6: Survey of Worldviews and Key Drivers

The final step in developing a whole-system change implementation strategy is to identify the worldviews and key drivers of the employee population. The purpose of this diagnostic is threefold:

(1) To customize the design of the communications surrounding the whole-system change initiative, particularly the compelling reasons for change, so that they align with the worldviews and key drivers of the employee and executive populations.

(2) To customize the methodology and content of the cultural transformation program so that they too align with the underlying drivers and worldviews of the employee population, and

(3) To provide executives and managers with personal feedback for coaching purposes.

The diagnostic tools used to uncover the worldviews or key drivers of the executive and employee population are the spiral dynamics assessment instruments. These instruments identify the degree of acceptance and rejection of eight basic worldviews. Table 9–2 provides an overview of the eight worldviews. Each worldview is represented by a color. The

Table 9-2 Spiral Dynamics Worldviews, Beliefs, and Key Personal Drivers

Worldview	Beliefs	Key Drivers/Personal Descriptors
TURQUOISE Holistic/whole system	Self is both distinct and a blended part of a larger, compassionate energetic whole.	I want to work on solving global issues for the sake of humanity and future generations.
	Everything connects to everything else in a harmonious ecological balance.	These problems can only be solved through multidisciplinary approaches.
	Energy and information permeate the earth's environment. There is an underlying order to chaos.	Keep day-to-day problems in perspective—don't sweat the small stuff.
	The world is a single, dynamic organism with its own collective mind.	Personally, I want to keep my life as simple as possible.
	Holistic, intuitive, and cooperative actions are to be expected.	We need time for daily personal reflection so that we can be responsive to what wants to emerge.
YELLOW Intellectual/ integrative	Life is composed of complex natural hierarchies and systems.	It is important to bring understanding to complexity.
	Competence, flexibility, spontaneity, and functionality have the highest priority.	Solving complex problems is important to me and helps society evolve.
	Make choices based on what is most appropriate to the situation and conditions.	Give me space for free thinking and systems analysis.
	Understand that chaos and change are natural.	Living my values is more important than gaining material possessions.
	Difficulties are opportunities for learning.	My life and my work are unified.
	I can only improve my life if I improve life for everyone.	I need to keep the big picture in mind when solving everyday problems.
		I strive to increase my competence.

Table 9–2 *Continued*

Worldview	Beliefs	Key Drivers/Personal Descriptors
GREEN Egalitarian/social	The human spirit must be freed from dogma and divisiveness. Feelings, sensitivity, and caring should supersede cold rationality. Care for the earth and spread resources and opportunities equally among all. Reach decisions through processes that emphasize reconciliation and consensus. We are all basically equal and share the same values.	I want to be an accepted member of the community. I need to communicate my feelings. It is important to pay attention to the feelings of others. Inequality and conflict should be avoided. We focus on the values we share. I seek opportunities for personal growth and development. It is important to have a spiritual outlook on life.
ORANGE Competitive/strategic	Change, competition, and advancement are inherent with the scheme of things. Optimistic, risk-taking, and self-reliant people deserve success. We prosper through the appropriate use of strategy and technology. We progress by learning nature's secrets and seeking out the best solutions for humans. Manipulate the earth's resources to create and spread the abundant good life.	I learn new things so I can outsmart the competition and be more successful. We need to measure progress. Make me accountable and I will deliver the results. Do the research and give me the numbers. What's the plan of action? I take calculated risks to get what I want. I bend the rules if necessary. I grab opportunities when they arise. Winning is important. Keep a sharp eye on competitors.

BLUE Organizing/ hierarchical	Bring order to chaos so that our collective lives can be improved. Sacrifice self to the transcendent cause. Sacrifice now to reap future rewards. Enforce codes of conduct based on tried and tested principles. Control impulsivity through guilt. Everyone has his or her proper place in society. Laws, regulations, and discipline are necessary for order and to build character and moral fiber.	We see benefits for everyone in obeying the rules. We keep our systems and processes functioning and well maintained. We are loyal and true to the cause. Loyalty will ultimately be rewarded by advancement in status. We keep our world in order through self-discipline. We like to finish what we start and keep things orderly. We act responsibly within the framework of rules and regulations that govern our status within the hierarchy.
RED Power/impulsive	The world is a jungle full of threats and predators, so be cautious and scheming in the way you deal with the world. It is important to break free from domination or constraint so I can please myself as I desire. Enjoy self to the fullest right now without guilt or remorse. Stand tall, demand respect, and call the shots. Conquer, outfox, and dominate those who could threaten my control and want what I have got.	I have to dominate to stay on top. I will have more power and get more respect if I can build my empire or enlarge my silo. It is difficult to trust those who are not in my circle. I am always alert to potential dangers. I sometimes react impulsively to satisfy my personal desires. I seek respect from peers but don't give a damn what anyone else thinks. I think it is important to avoid shame.

Table 9-2 *Continued*

Worldview	Beliefs	Key Drivers/Personal Descriptors
PURPLE Tribal/sacrifice	The world we live in is basically unsafe. We can live safely if we stick together in the confines of our "tribe." The group is always more important than the individual. Demonstrate allegiance to those who are responsible for the well-being of the tribe or "family." Preserve traditions and rituals to stay in harmony with the natural cycles of life on which we are dependent for our existence. Pay attention to the magic and mystical signs that emanate from the spirit world.	We stay close to those that we regard as family. We are loyal and faithful to those who protect our interests. We are willing to sacrifice our needs so that we can be part of a group that offers us protection. We look forward to the times we spend together in celebration and ritual because it strengthens our "family" ties. We tend to be superstitious when strange things happen that don't have a logical explanation. We are suspicious of strangers.
BEIGE Instinctive/survival	Survival is what life is about. Food, water, warmth, sex, and safety have priority over all else. Become part of a band to perpetuate life and survive. Live "off the land" opportunistically.	I stay alive by satisfying the physical urges of the body as and when I can. I stick with what works and develop life-preserving habits that increase the chances of my survival.

"beige" worldview (instinctive and focused purely on physiologic survival) is mainly confined to isolated bands living in the most remote parts of the earth and is not generally included as an option in the spiral dynamic diagnostic tools. It is included here for the sake of completion.

We can also use the key drivers of the employee population to characterize the organization's identity. Table 9–3 provides a snapshot image

Table 9–3 Employee Drivers and the Images they Create

Worldview	Employee Drives	Projected Image
TURQUOISE Holistic/whole system	Global awareness, holistic approach	They care about humanity and the earth.
YELLOW Intellectual/ integrative	Intelligent, flexible, and sees the big picture	They are creative, open to new ideas, and easy to work with.
GREEN Egalitarian/social	Caring and friendly	They are focused on building lasting and meaningful relationships.
ORANGE Competitive/ strategic	Effective, progress/success-driven	They get results that impact performance.
BLUE Organizing/ hierarchical	Reliable and dependable	They are sound and solid as a rock.
RED Power/impulsive	Powerful and fast	They can handle whatever comes along.
PURPLE Tribal/sacrifice	Rooted in tradition and history	They are always there for you.

that each worldview projects out into the world.[8] It is important that the principle drives of the employee population are congruent with, and support the type of business of the organization. For example, I want my bank to be reliable and dependable (blue), friendly and caring (green); I want my business advisor to be effective and focused on results (orange) while keeping the big picture in mind (yellow); and because I operate from yellow, I want the charities I support to focus on solving global problems (turquoise).

We can apply the same logic to the internal functions of the organization. As a CEO, I want my accounting department to be solid blue (reliable) with a tinge of yellow so they keep the big picture in mind. I want my sales team anchored in orange (results) with a tinge of green so they project a caring image to the customer. I want my researchers anchored in yellow (intellect) with a tinge of blue so their research can be relied upon. I want my top team anchored in yellow (big picture) with some turquoise (global awareness) and orange (focused on results) with all the other colors present so I get a diversity of worldviews to help me make decisions.

The underlying drivers of the employee populations of different countries can vary significantly. For example, there are palpable differences between worldviews of employee populations in Canada (green) and the United States (blue and orange). I once worked on a cultural transformation program for a multinational company based in Sweden, Finland, Germany, and Poland. Even though at that time I had not integrated spiral dynamics into my practice, the biases of the personal values of the employee populations in each of these countries showed up clearly in the CTT cultural values assessment. Cultural differences can

[8] Hans Versnel and Hans Koppenol. *Managing Drives.* Available at www.managementdrives.com.

significantly impact working relationships between different offices and factories in multinational companies.

In addition to the differences we find in employee worldviews based on country cultures, there are also differences in the worldviews found in specific industries. Banking and the world of finance tend to attract people with "blue" and "orange" worldviews, whereas public service tends to attract people with "blue" and "green" worldviews. This is true in all regions of the globe. These country and industry differences need to be identified and taken into account when designing cultural transformation and structural alignment programs for global corporations.

There are two more points I want to make about worldviews. Consultants and change agents that design cultural transformation programs for organizations and support leaders in implementing whole-system change projects should be self-actualized individuals who are anchored in yellow, and have mastered orange, blue and green thinking. The ability to see and appreciate the interplay of the different worldviews is essential. This is impossible without a yellow perspective. Those who are anchored in purple through green are unable to see the big picture because they cannot detach sufficiently from their worldviews. Their sense of identity is so wrapped up in their belief structures that they are unaware of their cultural myopia. This is why one needs to be anchored in the systems thinking approach of yellow to appreciate where people are and help them to get where they want to go.

Finally, it is important to recognize that the eight worldviews, like the seven levels of consciousness, are evolutionary in nature. At each new stage of development a new more comprehensive attitude is developed to the previous stage.

It should also be noted that red, orange, and yellow are individual worldviews, and purple, blue, green, and turquoise are community worldviews. A top team composed of individuals anchored mainly in the individual worldviews may have difficulty coalescing: They will be focused on power, winning, and using their intellects to get what they personally want. A top team composed of individuals anchored mainly in community worldviews may have difficulty adapting to new challenges: They will get bogged down in tradition, bureaucracy, and reaching consensus.

The relationship between "how" people think—the eight contextual intelligences or worldviews—and "what" people think or what motivates them—the seven levels of consciousness—is shown in Figure 9–2. We find that people with different worldviews have different priorities at each level of consciousness.

What people think about or consider important at a particular level of consciousness depends on what worldviews they hold. For example, at level 1 consciousness, beige focuses on physical survival; purple focuses on safety; red focuses on exploitation; blue focuses on control; and orange focuses on wealth. The reason for these differences is that

Levels

	Beige	Purple	Red	Blue	Orange	Green	Yellow	Turquoise
7							Wisdorm	Compassion
6						Environmental	Inter-dependence	Community
5					Creativity	Shared Values	Openness	Transpartncy
4				Purpose	Accoutability	Consensus	Continuous Learning	Information Sharing
3			Power	Status	Success	Acceptance	Competence	
2		Ritual	Domination	Discipline	Competitiveness	Open Communication		
1	Survival	Safety	Exploitation	Control	Wealth			
World-views	Beige	Purple	Red	Blue	Orange	Green	Yellow	Turquoise

Figure 9–2 Integration of worldviews with levels of consciousness

purple has mastered physical survival and is now concerned with safety; red has mastered survival and safety and now is focused on exploiting the world to get what he or she wants; blue has mastered survival and safety and has brought order to the anarchy and chaos created by red. With the mastery of survival, safety, and the order created by blue, orange's focus at level 1 is on building wealth. Green has a blind spot at level 1—anything to do with money is an anathema to green—whereas yellow and turquoise have mastered level 1—they are unconsciously competent at this level, so these issues are no longer on their minds.

Similarly, at level 3 consciousness we see that red is concerned about power; blue is concerned about personal status; orange is concerned about success; green is concerned about acceptance; and yellow is concerned about competence. Level 3 corresponds to the birth of the ego. Because beige has no distinct sense of self and purple's identity is subsumed into the tribe, these two worldviews do not give expression to ego consciousness. Red's ego is looking for respect by being dominant and powerful. Blue's ego is looking for differentiation and status in the hierarchy of authority. Orange's ego is focused on acheivement and winning. Green has a sensitive ego and seeks acceptance by being politically correct. Yellow has blended its ego with its soul and approaches differentiation and respect through competence and merit.

What we also notice from Figure 9–2 is that the span of each worldview is roughly concentrated across five levels of consciousness. Thus, orange is centered on level 3—success through professional growth—and is unable to think in terms of levels 6 and 7 consciousness—issues regarding the environment and social responsibility are not on the orange radar screen. Green on the other hand is centered on level 4—development through personal growth. Pure green finds it difficult to get along with pure orange because these two worldviews have completely different attitudes toward money and the environment. Green wants to save the environment; orange is ready to exploit it to create wealth.

From a Maslovian perspective, self-actualized individuals tend to be anchored in yellow. They have mastered their fears and have learned to minimize the impact on their lives of the shadow side of their egos.

Full-spectrum individuals tend to be anchored in yellow and/or turquoise and display some of the healthy aspects of the worldviews associated with purple, red, blue, orange, and green. A healthy orange is vital for business entrepreneurs.

As I have already stated, it is important to recognize that personal alignment and group-cohesion programs need to be designed to match the predominant worldviews of the participants. Whatever you want to do in these areas, red does not want to participate; blue wants the program focused on leadership and will only attend if the people in the room are at the same level; orange will only engage if they can see a direct benefit to their future success, and the programs are scientifically based; green cares less about science and more about exploring their personal emotions and feelings; yellow needs to see the bigger picture—the "why" of each element of the program, how the elements fit together, and the road map; turquoise wants to understand the program from a holistic or global perspective and the interplay of energies that are being called forth by different elements of the program.

It is also important to note that groups of individuals anchored in the purple to green spectrum find it difficult to reconcile their differences because their identities are constructed around their beliefs, and beliefs are always contextual. It is only when individuals and groups take on a yellow worldview that they develop the ability to shift from conscious belief-based decision making to values-based, decision making. That is why yellow and turquoise are able to understand the positions taken by those who are operating with purple through green worldviews—they recognize the underlying values.

As you can see, the advantage of examining an organizational culture from the seven levels of consciousness perspective and from spiral dynamics perspective is that it provides us with a deeper understanding of the organization's culture and values, and the worldviews and drivers of the leaders, executive population, managers, and staff.

The difference between the seven levels of consciousness model and the spiral dynamics model is that the former provides a means of understanding what is on people's minds—what they are thinking and what motivates them; whereas the latter provides a means of understanding how people think—it uncovers the underlying worldviews that drive their motivations.

The difference between these two models and all others that attempt to map values and consciousness is they have "built-in verticality": They are evolutionary in nature and provide a developmental blueprint for the evolution of human consciousness. If you know where you are as an individual or a group on the maps provided by these two models you know exactly what the next emergent evolutionary motivational challenge will be. These insights are of fundamental importance in engineering personal and social change and designing the habitats that support the evolution of group consciousness.

Step 7: Develop an Implementation Strategy

A strategy is a plan for achieving a specific outcome. It keeps everyone moving in the same direction towards the same goal. At this point in the whole-system change initiative, the CEO and leadership team have sufficient information to develop a detailed implementation program. They have compelling reasons for change; they have customized this communication so that it aligns with the worldviews and key drivers of the executive and employee population; they have a clear sense of collective direction—the vision and mission; they know their cornerstone values or principles; and they have a set of operational values and behaviors that guide their day-to-day decision making and actions.

Now, the consultant/change agent must assist the CEO and leadership team in making the vision, mission, values, and behaviors pervasive throughout the culture. As discussed in the previous chapter, there are three major components to the change process: personal alignment, group cohesion (values alignment and mission alignment), and structural alignment.

The purpose of the personal alignment and group-cohesion programs is to kick start the whole-system change process by focusing on the values alignment and mission alignment of the top team and the teams that report to the members of the top team. This group usually comprises between 50 and 100 executives. These executives are the guardians of the culture. They are the ones who must walk the talk if the culture is to change. Without their whole-hearted support there will be no whole-system change and no cultural transformation.

In larger organizations, it will be necessary to take the personal alignment and group-cohesion programs further down the executive chain. For budget reasons, the personal alignment and group-cohesion programs usually morph into a shorter, less resource-intensive values awareness programs as you move down the hierarchical chain of command (see stage 14).

It is important not to get locked into "the one right way" of implementing whole-system change. There are many paths to the summit. The most important rule is you have to begin where people are if you are going to lead them to where they want to go.

Step 8: Develop Objectives and Key Performance Indicators

Measurement matters. It is vitally important to set targets for the whole-system change initiative: not just performance improvements and bottom-line improvements, but also cultural and individual leadership improvements.

We can categorize key performance indicators into three types: "causal"—indicators that relate to values and behaviors; "output"—indicators that relate directly to performance such as efficiency and productivity; and "outcome"—indicators that relate to the end results such as profitability and shareholder value.

Causal targets are set for values and behavior improvement at both the group level (organization-wide and business units) and at the individual level. Indicators of values and behavior improvement at the organization-wide and business unit level include a decrease in cultural entropy, a reduction in potentially limiting values in the top ten current culture values, an increase in the alignment of personal values with the current culture values, and an increase in the alignment current culture values with desired culture values. All of these indicators are provided by the cultural values assessment. Indicators of values and behavior improvement among the leaders and executive population include a decrease in personal entropy generation (fear-based behaviors), a reduction in potentially limiting values, an increase in the number of matching values between the assessors and assessee, and a shift toward full-spectrum leadership consciousness. All these indicators are provided by the leadership values assessment (LVA).

"Output" targets refer to indicators of performance improvement such as productivity, efficiency, quality, innovation, creativity, and employee and customer satisfaction. These are lead indicators for the satisfaction of the outcome targets. "Outcome" targets refer to indicators of business improvement such as market share, profitability, and shareholder value. The basic premise is that changes in values and behaviors lead to performance improvements (outputs), which in turn lead to business improvements (outcomes).

Referring to the four-quadrant diagram, what we want to create are shifts in the internal quadrants of the individual and collective (shifts in intentions) that result in shifts in the external quadrants of the individual and collective (shifts in behaviors).

Table 9–4 identifies some of the most frequently used causal, output, and outcome performance indicators. The causal indicators are subdivided into key performance indicators (KPIs) for groups (organization-wide and business units) and individuals (leaders and executives). The outcome indicators are subdivided into KPIs for companies and government agencies.

Organizations have been measuring output and outcome KPIs for decades, usually as part of a balance scorecard program—output targets are usually referred to as "lead" indicators and outcome targets are usually referred to as "lag" indicators.

What is new and significant about Table 9–4 is the ability to accurately measure, against base-line data, year-by-year changes in the causal KPIs at the group and individual levels using the results of the CTT cultural values assessment (CVA) and the leadership values and behaviors assessment instruments (LVBA). Measuring and mapping the values of an organization and individual leaders on a regular basis to monitor and guide cultural change is known as values-management. Chapter 11 provides a detailed description of the process of values-management and the use of the CTT values assessment instruments for creating a dashboard of causal indicators of performance.

Values-management begins with the baseline cultural values assessment at the start of the whole-system change process. A second "reading" of the culture to map the changes in values is usually carried out once the implementation phase of the whole-system change process is well under way—approximately 12 months after the first cultural values assessment or 6 months after the start of the implementation phase.

Table 9–4   Key Causal, Output, and Outcome Performance Indicators

Causal KPIs	Output KPIs	Outcome KPIs

Groups[a]
Cultural entropy
Number of limiting values
Alignment of personal and
   current culture values
Alignment of current and
   desired culture values
Espoused values alignment
Cornerstone values alignment
Seven levels of consciousness
   alignment
	Employee satisfaction
	Customer satisfaction
	Productivity
	Efficiency
	Quality
	Effectiveness
		Corporations
		Shareholder value
		Profit
		Market share

Individuals[b]
Personal entropy
Limiting values
Matching values (assessor
   and assessee)
Consciousness alignment
Values and behavior
   alignment
		Government
		Measures of mission
		Assurance such as
		   coverage, range of
		   services, and
		   availability of
		   services

KPI: Key performance indicator.

[a] KPIs obtained from the cultural transformation tools cultural values assessment instrument (CVA).

[b] KPIs obtained from the cultural transformation tools leadership values and behaviors assessment (LVBA).

Organizations that practice values-management generally monitor their cultures every 9 to 12 months. It is desirable to monitor the values/behaviors of the executive population more frequently.

Implementation Phase

The implementation phase, shown diagrammatically in Figure 9–3, can take between 1 to 3 years depending on the size of the organization, the demands of other ongoing initiatives, budget restraints, and the appetite and level of commitment among the leadership group and executive population for whole-system change. The implementation process

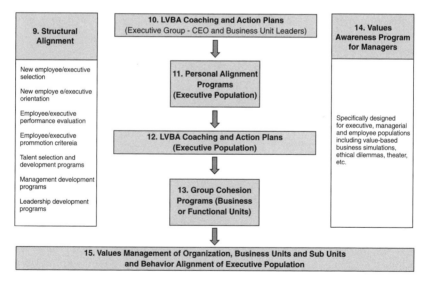

Figure 9–3   Whole-system change—implementation phase

begins with the definition of the content of the structural alignment process and the definition and design of the personal alignment, group cohesion, and values awareness programs.

Step 9: Structural Alignment

The purpose of the structural alignment program is to reconfigure the systems and processes of the organization so that they align with the vision, mission, values and behaviors of the organization. These processes form the underlying formal and informal behavioral reward systems that support the culture. They have a long-term impact on the culture because they are a materialization of "how things are done around here." The systems and processes that may need to be reconfigured are as follows:

- New employee/executive selection
- New employee/executive orientation
- Employee/executive performance evaluation
- Employee/executive promotion criteria
- Selecting talented performers for fast track development
- Leadership development programs
- Management training programs
- Values awareness programs

In large organizations, the structural alignment changes can take up to 2 to 3 years to implement. It is also useful at this stage to develop programs that directly address specific limiting values in the current culture such as a bureaucracy elimination program and/or an accountability promotion program.

Step 10: Leadership Values and Behaviors Assessment of the Senior Executive Group (Chief Executive Officer and Direct Reports), Coaching, and Action Plans

The first task of any cultural transformation program is to support the leadership team in living the values and behaviors. They must walk the talk, and they must display visible signs of changes in their behaviors if they are to avoid criticism and cynicism from the employee population.

The most common problem that leadership teams display is a lack of cohesion. Most often this is because they do not trust each other. Furthermore, there is no sense of shared mission and very few shared values. This results in silo-mentality or empire building, where leaders compete with each other for resources and power and there is very little sense of group cohesion or working for the common good. On the contrary, what we see in these situations is a strong focus on self-interest.

After the leadership team has spent several days together working on the vision, mission, values, and behaviors (see steps 2 and 3), they have generally begun to develop a greater sense of unity and respect for each other. The four-whys process brings the team together as they explore their collective values and their core motivations and get clear on the core business of the organization.

It is at this point we use the LVBA instrument together with a 2-hour individual coaching session to help the leadership team shift their behaviors. At the end of the coaching session, each member of the leadership team prepares a personal development plan that they share with each other in a behavioral alignment workshop. They then commit to meeting again with each other in 6 to 8 weeks to share progress with each other and offer constructive feedback. Through this process we are in effect making personal transformation mutually accountable.

The results from this process are almost instantaneous. We have seen the most hardened business types and bureaucrats begin to adopt new behaviors within days or weeks. There will always be a small percentage of people who find behavior change difficult or who are not significantly impacted by this process. These are usually people with deeply engrained limiting beliefs. To get past these difficulties, these people should be assigned a personal coach. Sometimes, with regular coaching, breakthroughs occur. Sometimes they do not. Those who cannot adjust will leave, often under their own volition.

Stages 11, 12, and 13: Personal Alignment Programs with the Executive Population, Group-Cohesion Programs in Intact Teams of Business or Functional Units and Subunits and Leadership Values and Behaviors Coaching with the Executive Population

These three programs (personal alignment, group cohesion, individual coaching) reinforce each other in bringing about a shift in the individual and collective behaviors of the executive population. Although the purpose of these programs is always the same, the content may change depending on the worldviews and key drivers of the executive population.

The focus of the personal alignment program is to support the executive population in their self-actualization. The leaders need to know themselves and to understand their core motivations. They need to identify their strengths, limiting beliefs, and future aspirations. They need to learn how to confront conflicts and how to challenge others, as well as how to communicate effectively, trust each other, release judgments, and give and take feedback.

When people leave the personal alignment program they are different from when they came in. They will have a clearer and more positive outlook of themselves and their work environment, a better understanding of themselves, and greater confidence and effectiveness in dealing with others.

Personal alignment programs can involve individuals from all parts of the organization because the focus is on self, not on the team. Alternatively, the personal alignment workshops can be carried out in intact teams: the top teams of the direct reports of the CEO, or the business unit or functional unit top teams, and the top teams of the subunits. The objective is to have as a minimum the top three layers of the executive population experience this program.

We build the bridge from personal alignment to group cohesion by having each individual who has experienced a personal alignment workshop carry out a LVBA similar to the top team. We want them to get feedback from their peers, subordinates, and managers on their operating values and their degree of alignment with the organization's espoused values and behaviors. We want them to see how they are coming across to others and how well they model the organization's values. This process involves a 2-hour coaching session and the preparation of a personal development program. Team members share their personal development programs with each other at a behavioral alignment workshop. To save costs, the coaching sessions are sometimes carried out in small groups. The CEO and his or her top team receive individual personal coaching as part of their feedback from the LVBA.

The main purpose of the group-cohesion workshop is to build trust, focus, clarity, and coherence among the team members. Team members who have experienced the personal alignment workshop and have prepared a personal development program come together in their intact teams to co-create a community of equals aligned around a shared vision, a shared mission and shared values.

The group-cohesion workshop helps each individual to understand how to work with group dynamics and see how his or her personal sense of mission aligns with the overall vision and mission of the group.

Participants leave the group cohesion program knowing clearly how their own sense of personal mission supports the organization's vision and mission. Without a clear line of sight between one's personal mission and the vision or mission of the organization, there can be no group cohesion, no commitment, and no enthusiasm. When we find meaning in our work we give our all.

The starting point of the group cohesion workshop is to provide the intact team with feedback on the degree of alignment between the current and desired culture of their business or functional unit—output from the CTT cultural values assessment. We want them to see their collective strengths and to understand the gaps between where they are now and where they collectively want to be. They need to know that they are collectively accountable for making this change. In addition to the group result, individual results are provided for each member of the team. The results of these assessments for each business and functional unit are essential for establishing a baseline from which progress can be measured against the performance improvement plan. The content of the group-cohesion workshop is customized for each business unit based on the results of the cultural values assessment.

The group-cohesion programs needs to begin with the top teams and cascade down through each of the business or functional units to at least the third layer of management. In small organizations, it may only be necessary to focus on the top echelons of management.

In large organizations, the depth to which we take the personal alignment and group-cohesion programs depends to a large extent on the results of the CTT cultural values assessment. If after examining the results of the assessment by grade or level we find a "crisis" culture (see Figure 6–16) then we would take these two programs as deep as possible into the organization. If on the other hand, the results of the cultural values assessment show that we are dealing with "shadow" culture (Figure 6–13), then we would focus our efforts on the top two or three echelons of the executive population. In the case of a "squeeze" culture (Figure 6–15) we would take a closer look at the causes of the high mid-level cultural entropy before deciding on the scope of these programs. The most difficult type of culture to deal with is the "denial" culture (Figure 6–14). Until the senior team recognizes its role in creating the high level of cultural entropy in the executive population, there is little that can be done. In a values-driven culture (Figure 6–17), we would once again focus our efforts on the senior echelons of the executive population.

The results of the CTT cultural values assessment are also used to determine the priority order of business units to be taken through the personal alignment and group-cohesion programs. We would focus on: (a) the groups with the highest levels of cultural entropy, and (b) the groups with the most energy for this work. What we are looking for are some early and significant wins to create a buzz of excitement in the organization.

Step 14: Values Awareness Program

At whatever level we stop the cascade of the personal alignment and group-cohesion programs, we replace it with a "value awareness" program and cascade it through the rest of the organization. The values awareness program is usually designed in two formats, a 1 or 2-day program for managers and a half-day or full-day intervention with staff. For staff it can be an extended meeting that forms part of their normal interactions with their managers or a one-day workshop specifically designed for each business or functional unit. In all cases, the values awareness program starts with an introduction by someone at least two levels senior to the group, who explains the compelling reasons for change, outlines the vision, mission, values and behaviors, explains the proposed structural alignment changes, and specifies the objectives and specific targets for the key values-management performance indicators.

The purpose of the values awareness workshop is to begin to inculcate the vision, mission, values and behaviors among the management population and employee base. Apart from the informational content, the program needs to give the participants the opportunity to explore their own values and understand the concept of values-based decision making through the discussion of ethical dilemmas or through a business simulation exercise.

One of the tools we have developed to raise managers' awareness of values-based decision making is the Values-Based Leadership: Business Simulation.

Teams of 4 to 5 are given the task of turning around an ailing company that is rapidly losing customers due to poor product quality and customer service. The results of a cultural values assessment showing the top ten current values of the company plotted against the Seven Levels of Consciousness model and Business Needs Scorecard are provided to the team at the start of the simulation so they can understand what is working and not working in the company culture.

The team's job is to bring the company back to profitability by building a values-driven culture that supports employee fulfillment, customer satisfaction, and shareholder value.

Every quarter, over a period of four years, the team has to: a) choose from a list of 23 projects, an initiative that will support the development of the company, b) respond to random events that take place in the company, in the market place, and in society, c) allocate overhead and production costs, and d) collect revenues from customers. At the end of each year the team produces a profit and loss account to see how well they have done.

Every decision the team makes shows up as a value on the simulation board in the Seven Levels of Consciousness model and the Business

Needs Scorecard. If the team chooses the right projects and responds appropriately to the events, they are able to build a profitable, full-spectrum organization with positive values at each level of consciousness and in every category of the Business Needs Scorecard.

The projects they choose from include: investment in quality improvement, re-engineering, team building, performance feedback, employee health and safety, customer relationship management, cultural transformation, social responsibility, work/life balance, strategic alliances, and so forth.

The events they have to deal with include topics such as brand image, corruption, promotion criteria for managers, quality improvement, removing layers of hierarchy, staff reduction, minority issues, environmental and human rights issues, and so forth.

The group dialogue that the simulation generates exposes the values that lie behind the team's decisions. It is clear at the end of each year how the team's values affect the culture, and how the culture affects business performance.

A short feedback/learning session occurs at the end of each year of the simulation, and a longer feedback/learning session takes place at the end of the simulation. The business simulation takes about 6 hours and usually involves groups playing in teams of four. The generic version of the business simulation is available in multiple languages.

The Values-Based Leadership: Business Simulation is customizable for specific industries and specific company situations. The starting point of the simulation can be based on the results of an actual cultural values assessment, and the events and projects can be designed to replicate industry-specific issues.

The simulation is also being used in universities to expose mature business students to the experience of values-based decision making in running a company. More information about this business simulation can be found at http://www.valuescentre.com/leaders/vbl.htm.

Another highly effective way of creating values awareness is to use theater, or theatrical techniques to illustrate through humor and story telling the dysfunctional behaviors of the current culture. Drama, as an art form, distills the scattered events and motives of organizational life into a compelling story that holds up a mirror to the system. When leaders, managers and staff are able to step outside their situation and see their own story, they have a chance to feel the weight and see the humor of their dysfunctional behaviors. They also have a chance to redirect the actors in such a way as to act out the values and behaviors of their desired culture. This demonstration of the undesirable behaviors and the modeling of the behaviors that support the desired culture can have a significant impact on shifting the culture of the organization.

Finally, it is important to recognize that in some situations the values awareness program should precede the personal alignment and group-cohesion programs with appropriate adjustments to the latter programs based on the content covered in the values awareness program. The main reason for this is to introduce and ground the concept of values-based decision making among the executive population. This is especially true when working with financial institutions where the belief-based "orange" competitive/strategic drive dominates. Where the "green" egalitarian/social or the "yellow" intellectual/integrative drives are dominant, there is more understanding of values-based decision making and more openness to embrace such concepts. The concept of values-based decision making is discussed in detail in the following chapter.

The last step of the whole-system change implementation process is to measure the results and develop a program of values-management. This is step 15 in Figure 9–2. I consider this topic to be so important that I have devoted all of Chapter 11 to a discussion of values management.

10

The Importance of Values-Based Decision Making

In the last chapter I put considerable emphasis on the importance of values-based decision making. This chapter explains why values-based decision making is essential for creating successful, healthy, and sustainable cultures. Before exploring values-based decision making, we need to understand the underlying dynamics of decision making.

The Four Vectors of Consciousness

There are four components to decision making (vectors of consciousness) that apply to all individuals and groups: data gathering, information processing, meaning making, and decision making (deciding on a course of action).

We use our five senses to gather data from the outside world—data gathering. We use our brain to integrate the data from the five senses into information packages—information processing. The mind then compares the incoming information package with the information packages stored in memory to find a match—meaning making. When it finds a match, it releases the instructions attached to the memory along with any emotional charge associated with the memory, which results in actions and behaviors—decision making. If the mind does not find a match, it uses reason and logic to formulate a response to the situation that seeks to exploit the situation to satisfy whatever motivations are currently occupying the mind. The response will be determined by many factors, the most important of which are the level of consciousness the mind is operating from and its predominant drivers.

The instructions that are attached to memory are learned from previous experiences. The most deeply engrained instructions are those we learned during childhood when our brains were still growing and our minds were still learning to understand and cope with the world. The purpose of the instructions associated with a memory is always to maintain or enhance the internal stability and external equilibrium of the individual. The instructions tell us how to survive, how to feel safe and secure, and how to safeguard our self-respect based on our individual experiences in our framework of existence.

The Five Modes of Decision Making

Over time, the human species has developed five modes of decision making. The difference between each mode of decision making is the source and emphasis we give to meaning making. There are five sources of meaning making: instincts, subconscious beliefs, conscious beliefs, values, and intuition.

Instinct-Based Decision Making

Instinct-based decision making takes place at the cellular level and is founded on learned DNA responses, principally associated with issues of survival. For example, babies instinctively know how to suckle, how to cry when their needs are not being met, and how to smile so they get attention. No one taught them how to do this. It is encoded in the species DNA.

In adult life, instinct-based decision making kicks in to help us survive and avoid dangerous situations. In certain situations, our instincts may cause us to put our life at risk to save the life of another. This is the principle mode of decision making of the "beige" instinctual/survival drive (from spiral dynamics) and is found in all creatures.

The main features of *instinct-based decision making* are (a) actions always precede thought—there is no pause for reflection between meaning making and decision making; (b) the decisions that are made are always based on past experiences—what our *species history* has taught us about how to survive and keep safe (maintain internal stability and external equilibrium). These instructions are encoded in the cellular memory of our DNA; and (c) we are not in control of our actions and behaviors. They are in control of us.

Subconscious Belief-Based Decision Making

In *subconscious belief-based decision making* we also react to what is happening in our world without reflection, but on the basis of personal memories rather than cellular (DNA) memories. In this mode of decision-making action also precedes thought. The action is often accompanied by the release of an emotional charge.

The emotional charge that accompanies the actions and behaviors in subconscious belief-based decision making can be positive or negative. Negatively charged emotions are associated with the satisfaction of the fear-based needs of the ego and lead to the display of potentially limiting behaviors—blame, internal competition, rivalry, caution, and so forth. Positively charged emotions are associated with the satisfaction of the needs of the soul and lead to the display of life-enhancing behaviors—openness, trust, cooperation, honesty, and so forth.

We know we are operating with subconscious fear-based beliefs when we get angry, upset, shout at people, or generally behave badly toward others or in a self-serving manner. What is driving this behavior is our subconscious fear-based beliefs around not having enough, not feeling safe and/or loved, and not being enough or not being respected—the subconscious fear-based beliefs associated with the first three levels of consciousness. These types of behavior are always accompanied by a pent up negative emotional charge.

The main features of *subconscious fear-based decision making* are as follows:

(1) Actions always precede thought: There is no gap between meaning making and decision making for reflection.

(2) The decisions that are made are always based on past experiences: What our *personal history* has taught us about how to maintain or enhance internal stability and external equilibrium at an individual level. This history is stored in our personal memory.

(3) We are not in control of our actions and behaviors. In this mode of decision making the only way we can get back into conscious control is either to release or bottle-up our emotions. Releasing helps us to return to rationality. Bottling-up creates stress and frustration. We are storing up negative emotional energy for future release.

(4) It is very personal. Others are not consulted to enhance meaning making and give support in reaching a decision.

(5) We are operating from the shadow side of the first three levels of consciousness: The behaviors we are displaying are based on deeply held beliefs about not being able to survive with

what we have (not having enough), not feeling safe (not belonging), and/or not being respected (not being enough). Subconscious fear-based decision making is the root cause of the majority of cultural entropy we find in organizations.

Conscious Belief-Based Decision Making

If we want to make rational decisions, we have to leave behind subconscious belief-based decision making and shift to conscious belief-based decision making. What allows us to make rational decisions is the pause we insert between meaning making and decision making. The pause allows us time for reflection and thought so we can use logic to understand what is happening and thereby make appropriate meaning out of the situation. In this mode of decision-making action follows thought. We have time to think about what decision to make, and we have time to discuss the situation with others and build consensus. We can only insert a pause between meaning-making and decision making if there is very little emotional charge associated with the memories that are triggered by events in the outside world.

Conscious belief-based decision making has one thing in common with subconscious belief-based decision making: It uses information based on past experiences (what we think we know) to make decisions about the future. It creates a future very much like the past. At best, the future we create is only incrementally different. We are using beliefs based on our past experiences to design our future experience.

Enabling leaders, managers, and employees to make the shift from subconscious belief-based decision making to conscious belief-based decision making is one of the main purposes of the personal alignment programs outlined in the previous chapter. We are attempting to uncover and release the limiting beliefs that cause emotional upset and prevent leaders, managers and employees from fully living their values. These are also the limiting beliefs that are the root cause of much of the cultural entropy we find in organizations.

Values-Based Decision Making

If we truly want to create the future we want to experience, we have to shift from conscious belief-based decision making to values-based decision making. That is not to say there is no place for conscious belief-based decision making based on logic and rational thinking. There is. However, all critical decisions need to pass the values test.

The question we need to ask when making a decision is the following: "Is this decision rational, *and* is it in alignment with our values?" If it is not in alignment with your values, you need to think again. A decision that is not in alignment with the organization's espoused values lacks integrity. A decision that is not in alignment with your personal values lacks authenticity. You cannot create personal or group cohesion by making decisions that lack authenticity and integrity.

We make values-based decisions so that we can create the state or feeling we want to experience.[1] If we value trust, then we need to make decisions that allow us to display and experience trust. If we value accountability, then we make decisions that allow us to display and experience accountability. When we make values-based decisions, we consciously create the future we want to experience. When we hold a vision, we consciously make decisions that keep us heading in that direction. When we have a mission, we consciously make decisions

---

[1] Antonio Damasio. *The Feeling of What Happens: Body and Emotion in the Making of Consciousness.* New York: Harcourt Brace & Co., 1999.

that support the attainment of that mission. In every case we are making decisions that help us consciously create the future we want to experience.

Values-based decision making is different from conscious belief-based decision making in that it de-emphasizes meaning-making based on past personal and species memories. In other words, we are not attempting to match up packages of information that represent our current experience with the packages of information stored in our personal and instinctual memory banks that release instructions based on past experiences. We are taking the packages of information that are created by the brain and we are examining them in our mind without any predetermined judgment about how we should respond. We are effectively saying to ourselves, "How can I respond to this situation in such a way that I am able to express my most deeply held values?" We are trying to let our values, not our beliefs, guide our behavior. Values are universal concepts that transcend all contexts and are soul-based. Beliefs on the other hand tend to be contextual and related to the satisfaction of the needs of the ego.

As already indicated, what is remarkable is that organizations that live by their values are among the most successful organizations on the planet. This is the key theme in most successful company turnarounds. It is one of the principle conclusions in Collins and Porras's book *Built to Last: Successful Habits of Visionary Companies.*[2] Successful long-lasting companies live their values. It is also one of our major findings based on 8 years of working with the seven levels of consciousness model and the cultural transformation tools. We have found that the most successful companies display full-spectrum consciousness: They operate with positive values at every level of consciousness. They have liberated their

---

[2] James C. Collins and Jerry I. Porras. *Built to Last: Successful Habits of Visionary Companies.* New York: HarperBusiness, 1994.

corporate souls. They make values-based decisions, and they know how to manage their fear-based beliefs.

Intuition-Based Decision Making

For most organizations, the shift from belief-based decision making to values-based decision making is already a stretch. The subsequent shift from values-based decision making to intuition-based decision making is for many a bridge-too-far. However, it is not a bridge-too-far for the more evolved leaders in an organization—those who have developed full-spectrum personal consciousness.

The principle characteristics of intuition-based decision making are as follows: (a) data gathering and information processing take place in the normal way; (b) judgment is suspended; no meaning making takes place, either subconsciously or consciously; (c) the mind is empty; thoughts, beliefs, and agendas are suspended; (d) the mind is free to make a deep dive into the mind-space of the collective unconscious; (e) after a short period, thoughts arise on the basis of an inner sense of knowing; and (f) the thoughts reflect wisdom; they focus on the common good; they are in alignment with our most deeply held values; and they give consideration to the long term. They reflect what is going on in our souls and the truth that wants to emerge.

What is different in this mode of decision making is that there is no conscious or subconscious attempt at meaning making, *and* there is no focus on the past or the future. The decision arises out of "presence" in the current moment. Beliefs lead to decisions based on past experiences. Values lead us to decisions based on the feelings we want to experience in the future. Intuition allows us to create a future based on the emergence of being. When we create the conditions that allow our minds to tap into the collective mind-space, our intuition informs us of what

wants or needs to emerge. This is the basis of the U-process used for collective decision making and described by Senge, Scharmer, Jaworski and
Flowers in *Presence: Human Purpose and the Field of the Future.*[3]

Conclusions

With this brief overview of the five modes of decision making, we can
clearly see why it is important for individuals and organizations to shift
from belief-based decision making to values-based decision making
and why they should try to eliminate subconscious fear-based decision making. This is why I called this book, *Building a Values-Driven
Organization*. To create such an organization requires us to constantly
focus on our individual and collective values. One of the ways to do this
is to practice values management.

[3] Peter Senge, C. Otto Scharmer, Joseph Jaworski, and Betty Sue Flowers.
Presence: Human Purpose and the Field of the Future. Cambridge: The Society
for Organizational Learning, 2004.

11

Values Management

Values management is the process by which an organization actively measures, monitors and responds to its causal indicators of performance in such a way that it adjusts its culture and way of being to sustain high performance (outputs) and meet its objectives (outcomes).

As we discussed in Chapter 9, there are three types of performance indicators—causal, output, and outcome indicators. The causal indicators are used to monitor the internal health of the organization by focusing on the energetic drivers of human performance—the values and behaviors of the executive and employee populations. They are called causal because they measure the motivations that drive the actions and behaviors of individuals and of the organization. All actions and behaviors are driven by internal motivations, and all internal motivations are driven by beliefs and values. As we have already discussed, to continually sustain high performance, four conditions must be met:

Personal alignment: The alignment of an individual's values and beliefs with their actions and behaviors.

Values alignment: The alignment of an individual's values with the group's values.

Mission alignment: The alignment of an individual's sense of purpose, mission or drivers with the group's stated purpose or mission.

Structural alignment: The alignment of a group's values and beliefs with their actions and behaviors as codified in the collective rules, laws, and processes of governance.

The process of values management enables us to measure the degree to which the four conditions are being met and how close they are to prime. Prime represents the healthiest possible state of the causal performance indicators commensurate with sustained mission assurance taking into account the levels of consciousness of the executive and employee populations. Prime is not an absolute measure. It can occur at any level of consciousness. In other words, prime can be experienced by groups with different worldviews; what is important is that the four vectors—personal alignment, values alignment, mission alignment, and structural alignment—are resonant with each other and reflect the same values and beliefs.

When the four quadrants are in alignment, the organization is as close as it can get to prime and cultural entropy is minimized. When the four quadrants are out of alignment, cultural entropy increases and the organization becomes dysfunctional. When this happens the energies of the executive population are consumed by the pursuit of self-interest (internal competition, power struggles, internal politics, empire building, and so forth) and the energies of the employee population are consumed by bureaucracy, cynicism and control.

Figure 11–1 shows what happened to the causal, output, and outcome performance indicators of a large financial organization as it brought the four quadrants into alignment by implementing a company-wide cultural transformation program. As the level of cultural entropy decreased (causal performance indicator), employee satisfaction increased (output

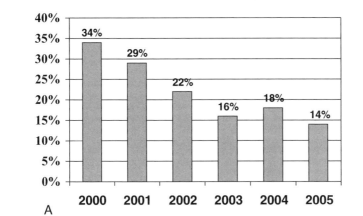

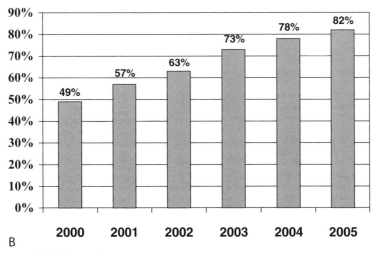

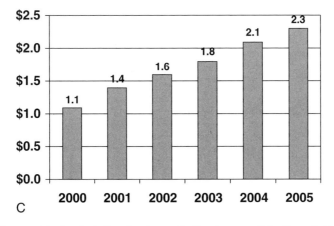

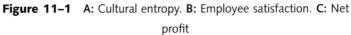

Figure 11–1 **A:** Cultural entropy. **B:** Employee satisfaction. **C:** Net profit

performance indicator), and profitability increased (outcome performance indicator).

Because the causal indicators are the principle drivers of outputs, which in turn drive outcomes, let us take a closer look at the key causal indicators of performance that are used in values management.

Key Values-Management Performance Indicators

As discussed in Chapter 9, there are two categories of values-management indicators—indicators that map the collective values and consciousness of groups (culture), and indicators that map the individual values and consciousness (personality) of the executive and employee populations. The individual values of the executive population significantly impact the collective values of the organization.

The principle instrument for measuring the values and consciousness of a group is the cultural values assessment (CVA). The CVA allows us to measure the collective values and consciousness of a group. The principle instruments for measuring the values and consciousness of individuals is the leadership values assessment (LVA) and the leadership values and behaviors assessment (LVBA).

Group Performance Indicators

The key causal indicators of group performance derived from the CVA are shown in Table 11–1. Also shown in this table are five measures of development for each indicator as they evolve toward prime. These measures are defined in the following manner:

Table 11–1 Key Values-Management Performance Indicators Derived from a Cultural Values Assessment

Key Performance Indicators	Measures	Critical Issues	Serious Issues	Significant Issues	Minor Issues	Prime
Cultural entropy	Proportion of votes for potentially limiting values in the current culture (%)	40% or more	30% to 39%	20% to 29%	10% to 19%	Less than 10%
Limiting values	Number of potentially limiting values in the top ten current culture values (no.)	4 or more	3	2	1	0
Matching personal and current culture values	Number of matching personal and current culture values in the top ten (no.)	0	1	2	3	4+

Table 11-1 *Continued*

Key Performance Indicators	Measures	Critical Issues	Serious Issues	Significant Issues	Minor Issues	Prime
Matching current culture and desired culture values	Number of matching current and desired culture values in the top ten (no.)	0 or 1	2	3 or 4	5 or 6	7 or more
Espoused values	Proportion of votes for each espoused value in the current culture (%)	0% to 9%	10% to 19%	20% to 29%	30% to 39%	40% or more
Cornerstone values	Proportion of votes for each cornerstone value in the current culture (%)	0% to 9%	10% to 19%	20% to 24%	25% to 29%	30% or more

Prime: High performance

Minor issues: Some problems that can easily be remedied

Significant issues: Problems that are causing significant malfunction in specific areas

Serious issues: Serious systemic problems affecting long-term viability and requiring pervasive responses

Critical issues: Critical systemic problems affecting short-term viability and requiring immediate action

Table 11–2 provides a dashboard of the first four causal key performance indicators listed in Table 11–1 for the company Flexite. The data supporting this table can be found in Figures 4–1 and 4–2. The indicators show that there are significant issues with the cultural entropy and critical issues with the number of limiting values in the current culture. The numbers of matching values are also at the critical level. The company is operating far from prime.

Table 11–3 shows a typical values-management dashboard for the employee population of a large bank for the period 2000 to 2005. What we see here is relatively poor performance from 2000 to 2002, with significant improvements beginning to happen in 2003 as the organization begins to focus on its culture and starts to seriously introduce a program of values-management.

Table 11–4 presents the seven levels of consciousness perspective on the large bank over the same period. The performance indicators are calculated by measuring the difference between the percentage of positive values in the current culture and the percentage of positive values in the desired culture at each level of consciousness for the overall employee population. A plus sign (+) indicates an excess of values in the current culture compared with the desired culture at a specific level of consciousness, and a negative sign (−) indicates a lack of values in the current culture compared with the desired culture at a specific level of

Table 11-2 Key Values-Management Indicators for Flexite (see Figures 4–1 and 4–2)

Key Performance Indicators	Measures	Critical Issues	Serious Issues	Significant Issues	Minor Issues	Prime
Cultural entropy	Proportion of votes for potentially limiting values in the current culture (%)			Significant issues (28%)		
Limiting values	Number of limiting values in the top ten current culture values (no.)			Critical Issues (5)		
Matching personal and current culture values	Number of matching personal and current culture values in the top ten (no.)			Critical Issues (0)		
Matching current culture and desired culture values	Number of matching current and desired culture values in the top ten (no.)			Critical Issues (1)		

Table 11–3 Dashboard of Key Values-Management Performance Indicators for a Large Bank

Key Performance Indicators	2000	2001	2002	2003	2004	2005
Cultural Entropy	42%	39%	38%	21%	15%	15%
Limiting values	6	5	5	3	1	1
Matching personal and current culture values	0	0	0	2	3	3
Matching current and desired culture values	0	0	1	3	4	5
Espoused value (accountability)	12%	15%	14%	24%	34%	35%
Cornerstone value (profit)	41%	39%	39%	34%	34%	34%

Table 11–4 Seven Levels of Consciousness Dashboard for a Large Bank

Levels of Consciousness	2000	2001	2002	2003	2004	2005
7	−6%	−5%	−4%	−3%	−2%	−2%
6	−9%	−8%	−7%	−5%	−4%	−3%
5	−14%	−14%	−15%	−10%	−5%	−4%
4	−10%	−9%	−10%	−5%	−3%	−1%
3	+3%	+6%	+4%	+3%	+4%	+3%
2	−13%	−8%	−6%	−5%	−3%	−3%
1	+12%	+7%	+6%	+6%	+7%	+5%

Table 11-5 Seven Levels of Consciousness Key Performance Indicators

Key Performance Indicator	Measure	Critical Issues	Serious Issues	Significant Issues	Minor Issues	Prime
Seven levels of consciousness	Difference in proportion of votes for positive values between current culture and desired culture (%)	–9% or lower	–6% to –8%	–3% to –5%	–2% to –1%	0% or higher

Current Culture /
Desired Culture Gap

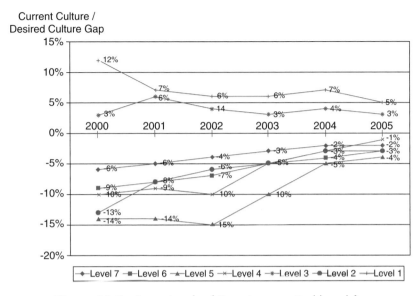

Figure 11–2   Seven Levels of Consciousness Dashboard for
a Large Bank

consciousness. A plus sign (+) therefore indicates the degree of mastery of the level of consciousness, and a negative sign (−) indicates the degree of lack of mastery of the level of consciousness. A graphic representation of Table 11–4 is provided in Figure 11–2. This diagram shows a steady reduction, over time, in the gap between the current culture and desired culture for each level of consciousness. Table 11–5 shows the five measures of development for this indicator.

Another example of a seven levels of consciousness dashboard this time from Flexite, is shown in Table 11–6. The graphic output for this data is shown in Figure 4–3.

We see from Table 11–4 that the large bank, like Flexite, has been good at focusing on the bottom line (level 1) and the systems and processes that drive performance (level 3). The bank has not been good at

Table 11-6 Seven Levels of Consciousness Dashboard for Flexite (see Figure 4–3)

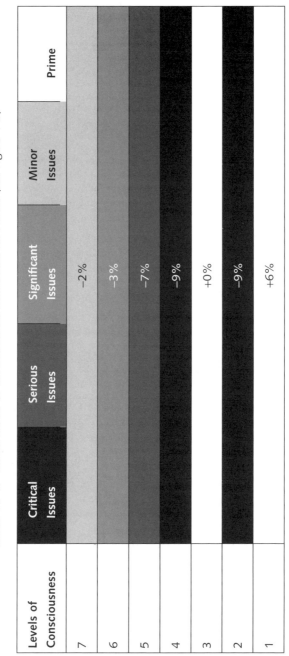

Levels of Consciousness	Critical Issues	Serious Issues	Significant Issues	Minor Issues	Prime
7			−2%		
6			−3%		
5			−7%		
4			−9%		
3			+0%		
2			−9%		
1			+6%		

employee and customer relationships (level 2), employee empowerment (level 4), internal cohesion (level 5), and strategic alliances (level 6). We see from Table 11–3 that the company was suffering from significant overall dysfunction—high cultural entropy and a low number of matching values. As cultural entropy was reduced, the number of matching values increased, and the gap between the percentage of positive values in the current culture and the percentage of values in the desired culture at each level of consciousness reduced.

The bank began to tackle its employee and customer satisfaction (level 2) issues in 2000/2001 and was making significant progress by 2003. It began to tackle its empowerment issues (level 4) in 2002/2003, and by 2005 had practically mastered this level of consciousness. By this time, the cultural entropy had reduced to 15% and there was only one limiting value in the current culture.

Even though the bank did not specifically address the value gaps at levels 6 and 7, there was a gradual alignment at these levels of consciousness as the organization concentrated on improving levels 2 and 4. Table 11–4 shows that the main focus of the values management initiatives in 2006 should be on continuing to improve the alignment at levels 2 and 4, and tackling the internal cohesion issues at level 5. The bank should explore what it might do to achieve a better alignment at level 6 by building strategic alliances and/or focusing on employee fulfillment.

The seven levels of consciousness dashboard (Table 11–4) provides a map of the degree of values alignment of the employee population no matter what levels of consciousness and underlying drivers the executives and employees are operating from. It is a true, dynamic, and detailed measure of consciousness alignment. The key performance indicators in Table 11–3, on the other hand, map the overall degree of cultural dysfunction and overall degree of cultural alignment of the organization, as well as the degree to which specific "value" targets are being met.

Table 11–7   Key Values-Management Performance Indicators by
Business Units of a Large Bank in 2002

Key Performance Indicators	Company	Retail	Capital Markets	Loans	Support
Cultural entropy	22%	19%	38%	15%	21%
Limiting values	2	2	5	1	2
Matching personal and current culture values	2	3	0	3	2
Matching current and desired culture values	3	3	1	6	3
Espoused value (accountability)	24%	24%	24%	30%	23%
Cornerstone value (profit)	24%	25%	34%	25%	21%

If we drill down into the results of the CVA for the large bank, we see that the overall dysfunction and values alignment issues are different in each business unit. Table 11–7 shows a snapshot of the key values-management performance indicators in 2002. We see from this dashboard that the capital markets business unit is not doing as well as the other business units. The only redeeming feature of the capital markets

Table 11-8 Seven Levels of Consciousness Alignment for Specific Business Units of a Large Bank in 2002

Levels of Consciousness	Company	Capital	Loans
7	−4%	−4%	−2%
6	−7%	−7%	−5%
5	−8%	−15%	−4%
4	−9%	−10%	−2%
3	+4%	+4%	+4%
2	−4%	−6%	−2%
1	+6%	+6%	+3%

business unit is its strong focus on profit. We also see in Table 11–7 that the loans business unit has the best degree of alignment.

Table 11–8 shows the results of the capital markets and loans business units from the seven levels of consciousness perspective in the year 2002. It is immediately noticeable that the employees in the capital markets business unit are not aligned with their desired culture. We also see that the employees in the loans business unit are closely aligned with their desired culture and are close to mastering levels 2, 4, and 7, having already mastered levels 1 and 3.

The poor performance of the capital markets business unit from a values-management perspective was holding back the progress of the whole company. Consequently, the bank replaced the vice president of the capital markets business unit, Jim Mason, with George Williams[1] at

---

[1] Jim Mason and George Williams are fictitious names.

Table 11–9 Evolution of Seven Levels of Consciousness Alignment in
Capital Markets

Levels of Consciousness	2002	2003	2004	2005
7	–4%	–3%	–2%	–2%
6	–7%	–5%	–4%	–3%
5	–15%	–10%	–5%	–4%
4	–10%	–5%	–3%	–1%
3	+4%	+3%	+4%	+3%
2	–6%	–5%	–3%	–3%
1	+6%	+6%	+7%	+5%
	VP Jim Mason	VP George Williams		

VP, vice president.

the end of 2002. This resulted in a rapid turnaround in values alignment indicators in this business unit.

Table 11–9 shows the evolution of seven levels of consciousness alignment indicators in the capital markets business unit from 2002 to 2005. George Williams was able to shift the culture of this department from 2003 onward because of his strong personal values-alignment.

Individual Performance Indicators

The key indicators of individual performance that are derived from the LVA are shown in Table 11–10 along with a description of how the

Table 11–10 Key Values Management Performance Indicators Derived from a Leadership Values Assessment

Key Performance Indicators	Measure	Critical Issues	Serious Issues	Significant Issues	Minor Issues	Prime
Personal Entropy	Proportion of votes for potentially limiting values of the leader reported by the assessors (%)	21% or more	11% to 20%	6% to 10%	3% to 5%	0% to 2%
Limiting values	Number of limiting values in the top ten values reported by assessors (no.)	4 or more	3	2	1	0
Matching Values	Number of matching top ten values between assessors and leader (no.)	0	1	2	3	4+
Consciousness Alignment	Proportion of matching "dots" per level for all levels of consciousness (%)	0% to 40%	50%	60%	70%	80% or more

indicators are calculated. Also shown are the five measures of develop-ment for each indicator. You will recall from Chapter 7 that the LVA is a feedback instrument that allows leaders to compare how they see them-selves against how their colleagues see them.

In addition to these indicators of individual performance, the LVBA also allows us to score the degree to which the assessors believe the leader is living the espoused values of the organization by measuring their behaviors. The dashboard for the behavior part of the leadership values and behaviors assessment is shown in Table 11–11.

A comparison of the individual dashboard for Jim Mason (2002) and George Williams (2003) is shown in Table 11–12, which shows clearly the significant differences in leadership styles of Jim Mason (the old leader) and George Williams (the new leader). Jim Mason has signifi-cant, serious, or critical issues on every measure, whereas George Williams has only minor issues or is operating at prime. George is sig-nificantly better at accountability than he is at teamwork and trust. These are the two areas he should focus on as he continues to improve his lead-ership style.

Since the behavioral assessment (BA) is easy to administer, leaders can use it on a regular basis (quarterly) to find out from their colleagues how well they are doing. The LVA, which involves an individual or group-coaching session, is more often used on an annual basis. The annual coaching session should be used as an opportunity to review the leader's development plan and refresh the targets for the coming year.

Values Management Software

The values-management process described in this chapter has been auto-mated so that it can be used as an online dashboard for organizations and individuals. The group and the individual perspectives are integrated

Table 11-11 Key Values-Management Performance Indicators Derived from a Leadership Values and Behaviors Assessment

Key Performance Indicator	Measures	Critical Issues 0 to 39	Serious Issues 40 to 49	Significant Issues 50 to 69	Minor Issues 70 to 89	Prime 90+
Specific value alignment	Average score of assessors (out of 100) for three or four behaviors that support each value.					

Table 11–12 Comparison of Values Management Performance Indicators for Jim Mason and George Williams Derived from Leadership Values and Behavior Assessment

Values Management Performance Indicator	Jim Mason	George Williams
Personal entropy	14%	3%
Limiting values	4	1
Matching values	1	4
Consciousness alignment	40%	80%

Value	Behaviors	Jim Mason	George Williams
Accountability	Takes responsibility for actions	52	94
	Admits mistakes, learns from them and takes corrective action	43	95
	Does what he/she says and lives up to his/her commitments	44	92

Value score	94	46
Teamwork	Actively contributes and shares responsibility for results	84	45
	Respects the opinions of others and listens attentively	75	51
	Asks for input and feedback from team members	74	45
Value score	78	47
Trust	Is open and candid	85	45
	Treats others with dignity and fairness	79	51
	Operates with integrity and supports colleagues	84	45
Value score	83	50
Overall values alignment score	85	48

so that a specific leader or manager can easily access his or her unit's per-formance indicators and his or her personal performance indicators. The top leaders can drill down to any level of the organization to monitor the degree of values alignment in a specific business unit, department or section. The shading used in this chapter is indicative of the colors that are used in the values management software. The colors allow the user to quickly identify the weakest areas of the organization from a values management perspective. Graphic outputs for time-series data can also be generated by the software. For more information on this software please refer to the Appendix.

12

Integrating Appreciative Inquiry

In Chapter 9, I outlined the basic framework we have developed for implementing whole system change. In particular, I drew attention to the importance of values and behaviors.

Based on years of experience of working with individuals and groups, transformation is seen to happen when people have new, meaningful conversations they have never had before, either one-on-one or in small groups. The process of whole-system change creates a number of opportunities for transformational conversations:

(1) When the leadership group uses the *four-whys process* to revisit or develop a new vision, mission and values for the organization.

(2) When the individual and collective values assessment results are debriefed with the leadership group.

(3) During the leadership group's discussion on their core motivations.

(4) During the leadership group's discussion on core business.

These types of conversations clarify and align the intentions of the leadership group. Another important conversation that needs to occur is translating the espoused values of the organization into specific behaviors that reflect the organizational context. *Appreciative inquiry* is one of the best technologies available for this task. The advantages that appreciative inquiry brings are as follows:

(1) It structures and focuses the conversation, and
(2) Just like the cultural values assessment, it gives employees and other stakeholders a voice in defining the parameters that will guide the future evolution of the organization.

Appreciative inquiry is a powerful technique for creating a positive future. It focuses on enhancing what is working rather than dwelling on what needs to be fixed. It affirms and builds on what is positive and strong about an organizational culture—what gives it life. It galvanizes people's energies by involving them in the process of defining the parameters that will guide the future evolution of the organization.

The appreciative inquiry process was developed by David Cooperrider and others at the Weatherhead School of Management (Case Western University, Cleveland, OH). The original impetus came from Cooperrider's work on his doctoral dissertation as he worked through an organizational analysis of a hospital. He found a high level of positive correlation between innovation and opportunities for equal voice. As his research continued, he discovered connecting practices and philosophies that grounded his work in a new theory and framework.

The theoretical basis for appreciative inquiry rests on the concept of social constructionism. The underlying beliefs of social constructionism are that reality is formed through conversation and story telling, that language and communication facilitate meaning making, and that knowledge is generated and passed on through social interaction. In its basic form, appreciative inquiry is a formalized process for designing powerful conversations.

The way we use appreciative inquiry to uncover the behaviors that support the espoused values is as follows. Having developed a short-list of values with the leadership group (or with the larger employee population), we bring together focus groups that represent a general cross-section of the employee population. The purpose of the focus group is to uncover the behaviors that support the values using an interview process based on an appreciative inquiry protocol.

The following box provides a short example of such a protocol inquiring into the value of accountability:

Preamble: As we interact with each other in attempting to build a great company, it helps to periodically stop and question what we have become. Do we still enjoy working in this organization? Do we have a sense of shared purpose? Do we have a sense of shared values? Such an inquiry helps us refocus our personal energy and passion and align it with the energy and passion of others. By working together openly and honestly on this inquiry we can improve our company and build a shared commitment to our collective future.

Basic Values Question [Accountability]

Tell a story about a time when you experienced a sense of *accountability* working in [company name] or another organization. Describe the situation. What were you doing? Who was with you? What was happening? How did your sense of accountability make you feel? How did others react? What was the most memorable aspect of this experience of accountability for you?

Continued

> Think of a time 5 years from now when executives, managers and employees in [company name] have *accountability* as one of the top Current Culture values. Describe what would be happening in the organization. What would it look like? How would it be different? What behaviors would you be seeing? How would you recognize accountability when it occurred?

Each focus group is split into pairs, and participants then interview each other using the interview protocol. Each interviewer takes notes as they interview their partner. The interviews can last from 30 minutes to an hour, depending on the length of the protocol. After each person has been interviewed, the focus group reconvenes and the results of the paired conversations are shared. The common behavioral themes resulting from interviews around the values are identified and recorded. When all the focus groups have met, the results are compared, and the behaviors associated with each value are finalized.

What is fascinating about the process is that it formally evokes storytelling. Many of the stories that emerge have a strong positive emotional content. These are the stories that people remember. Because the interview protocol encourages storytelling, it allows people to relate to each other and share their knowledge and experiences even though they may be at different levels in the organization. I remember once, by accident, pairing the chief executive officer (CEO) of a company with a janitor. To my surprise and pleasure, they had a very meaningful conversation. They were able to relate to each other through the energetic content of their stories.

What happens during the interview is that people get in touch with the positive emotions they experienced in the past when they lived a particular value. The value becomes real for them because of the remembered emotional content. They are able to verbalize what it felt like to experience a value, and can easily recall the behaviors that were taking place when the value was being lived.

Although we mostly use appreciative inquiry techniques for identifying the behaviors that support the chosen values of an organization, appreciative inquiry can be used either in parallel or as an alternative to the four-whys process for defining the vision and mission of an organization. This is only possible in situations where the leadership group is willing to share the formal process of defining the parameters that will guide the future evolution of the company.

Generally speaking, I have found that corporate leaders, particularly those with strong "red," "blue," or "orange" worldviews, feel uncomfortable involving the whole organization in such a process. Their belief structures are such that they are unwilling to share the power they have accumulated for themselves or let others control their destiny. Both "red" and "orange" are "I"-centered worldviews, and "blue" is based on hierarchies of dependency. Thus, in all three cases, a "democratic" approach that involves hearing the voices of all members of the group may not be a viable alternative.

The full appreciative inquiry process is described in several publications, including *Appreciative Inquiry: Rethinking Human Organization Toward a Positive Theory of Change*.[1] Further information can be found at http://appreciativeinquiry.cwru.edu/.

---

[1] David L. Cooperrider, Peter F. Sorensen Jr., Diana Whitney, and Therese F. Yaeger, eds. *Appreciative Inquiry: Rethinking Human Organization toward a Positive Theory of Change*. Champaign, IL: Stipes Publishing, 2000.

13

Integrating Resilience

The steady stream of natural and man-made disastrous events (hurricanes, tsunami, terrorism, civil wars) experienced throughout the world in the last few years has stimulated a great deal of interest in both sustainability and resilience. The dialogue has expanded to include not only psychological, social, and ecological approaches to sustainability and resilience, but also organizational, institutional, and national approaches. Resilience and sustainability have emerged as important frameworks for developing our personal, communal, and organizational capacities to withstand shocks, anticipate risks, and remain fully operational under conditions of extreme or prolonged duress while preserving our natural life-support systems.

Because of the increased frequency and scale of these extreme natural and man-made events, our current global operating reality seems less certain and less predictable than it did a few decades ago. We operate in an increasingly complex interconnected world that is becoming more difficult to predict.

Prominent insurance companies that have successfully operated for the last 100 years on probabilistic risk models are seriously questioning if those same models can still be used reliably to support underwriting. They are recognizing the need to take into account the low probability, extreme events such as global warming that could quickly overwhelm the adaptive capacity of our societal systems. Insurance risk teams are becoming alarmed by the "slow burn risks"—the systemic challenges arising out of incremental globalization changes that fall outside our line of sight because of our failure to consider the potential whole-system impacts of the accumulation of these incremental systemic changes. When these incremental changes reach a tipping point, they can have a significant impact, both positive and negative, on the internal stability and external equilibrium of our organizations and societies. Our increasingly complex, networked world is forcing us to take a more holistic view of the risks we face personally, organizationally, and nationally.

Consequently, IBM now offers "on demand" enterprise services to their clients backed up by a "business resilience" offering to keep the enterprise services working under all conditions. HP promotes the concept of the "adaptive enterprise" and Nortel features the "collaborative enterprise" as their tag lines. Booz Allen Hamilton offers "enterprise resilience" and "business assurance" service offerings to their diverse mix of government and commercial clients. Each of the consulting groups, in their own brand-aligned fashion, is seeking to reassure their clients that risk, change, and complexity can be confidently managed while sustaining growth and profitability. The prevailing trends are clear and compelling; accelerating change, deepening complexity, and growing systemic risks *are* the new "operating reality."

The reason why the integration of resilience-based models into our organizations, institutions and nations poses a significant challenge is because we process data linearly and mainly operate in hierarchical, bureaucratic cultures that cannot handle complexity or rapid change. Our organizations, institutions and nations have not yet developed the ability to be adaptive (level 4 consciousness). They are bogged down in high levels of cultural entropy.

At their core, resilience programs that build long-term sustainability are about enhancing the adaptive capacity of an organization (level 4 consciousness) and creating a culture of coordination, cooperation, and collaboration (level 5 and level 6 consciousness). Just as adaptability is a functional and operational prerequisite for overcoming shocks, the ability and willingness to cooperate, coordinate, and collaborate are cultural prerequisites for organizational and institutional resilience. In an increasingly complex and connected world, the resilience issue does not end at the boundary of the organization; it involves the intricate web of relationships and whole-system interdependencies that are part of the framework of existence of modern organizations.

The seven levels of consciousness model with the insights it brings on values alignment, cultural entropy, and full-spectrum sustainability, is an essential framework for evaluating the cultural resilience of our organizations and institutions. Blending the cultural transformation (CTT) tools and a whole-system approach to cultural transformation with resilience and adaptive capacity building techniques is essential for creating long-term resilience.

What has become clear over the past few years is that the emergent systemic risks that organizations face cannot be reliably identified within the current silo mentalities that exist in our organizations, nor are silos suitable for managing resilience programs. Organizations of all types are migrating mission critical business processes to information technology platforms that can be accessed from anywhere in the organization. Managing and maintaining these systems require a culture of cooperation, coordination, and collaboration across all parts of the organization.

It is becoming increasingly clear that what has been missing up to this point in the evolving resilience discussion is the role of culture in building sustainable, complex adaptive systems that are able to thrive in the new risk-intensive global operating environment. Indeed, recent risk-management performance-benchmarking studies indicate that many medium and large commercial and government organizations are not considering cultural issues at all in the design of their resilience programs.

Dealing with this missing link is a fundamental challenge we must address if we are to build truly sustainable organizations and institutions that are able to perform and provide services under duress. To this end, the concept of values-management, discussed in Chapter 11, is a timely innovation that allows organizations and institutions to monitor their cultural resilience by regularly monitoring their operating values and identifying high levels of cultural entropy. Wherever cultural entropy is high, resilience is low.

The following paragraphs provide a summary roadmap for conducting an enterprise-wide resilience survey and developing an enterprise-wide resilience implementation strategy.

Resilience Diagnostic

The resilience diagnostic includes a whole-system mapping of the organization's operational footprint, including critical network alliances, core business value chains, key business processes, strategic operational nodes, critical operational nodes, important assets, historical threats, and current high-impact risk issues associated with key business areas. The objective is to assess the organization's core capabilities with regard to managing historical risk patterns and current low probability, high-impact risks that may not yet be on the organization's radar screen.

Core capability domains include the following:

- Risk management
- Crisis management
- Business continuity planning
- Security and safety
- Corporate social responsibility and sustainability

Enabling capability domains include the following:

- Cultural values assessment and whole-system change capacities
- Values-management systems
- Performance-management systems
- Leadership development programs
- Decision support architecture

Cultural Diagnostic

The cultural diagnostic includes a CTT cultural values assessment to identify the degree of values alignment and level of cultural entropy in the organization and in each business or functional unit. The objective is to monitor the operational values and identify the areas of high cultural entropy that could impact the resilience of the organization under times of duress—the weakest areas of the organization.

Resilience and Culture: Gap Analysis

The resilience diagnostic is compared with the cultural diagnostic to identify which of the core business chains is at most risk from a cultural, structural, and operational perspective.

Identify Quick Wins

The results of the resilience and cultural diagnostic studies will bring to light both short- and long-term opportunities for enhancing the resilience of the organization and increasing the organization's adaptive capacity. Quick-win opportunities should be identified and implemented.

Identify Resilience Strategic Goals and Objectives

Based on the results of the diagnostic studies, the gap analysis and the vision and mission of the organization, identify the strategic goals and objectives for enhancing the resilience of the organization and its high-value interdependent networks.

Develop an Implementation Road Map

The implementation road map will include the following:

(1) Cultural changes that focus on (a) lowering the cultural entropy of the organization and (b) building an enhanced capacity for cooperation, coordination and collaboration—group cohesion;

(2) Structural changes that ease the flow and processing of information in times of threat or duress;

(3) Operational changes that reduce risks and lead to more agile and adaptive responses to changes in the organization's external and internal operating environment; and

(4) Performance-monitoring changes that provide early warnings of potential internal and external threats, risks, or weaknesses, including values management.

If a comprehensive resilience baseline diagnostic is not performed initially as part of a whole-system change effort, the cultural diagnostic needs to include some form of risk and resilience interview survey. This survey, together with the cultural values assessment, should be used to identify areas where cultural entropy and significant risks combine to create resilience "hot spots." Scenario-based tabletop simulations that explore these hot spots can be used to help organizations test existing decision-support and collaboration processes under complex event sequences.

14

Integrating the EFQM Excellence Model

The Emergence of Excellence in Europe

This concluding chapter describes an example of a whole-system approach to organizational transformation developed by the Centre for Integral Excellence at Sheffield Hallam University in the United Kingdom. The approach brings together the European Foundation for Quality Management Excellence model (EFQM) and the seven levels of consciousness model in an integral, whole-system, evaluation process.

The European Foundation for Quality Management is a not-for-profit foundation set up in 1989 by chief executive officers (CEOs) of 14 prominent European companies including British Telecomm, Dassault Aviation, AB Electrolux, Fiat, KLM, Nestlé, Philips Electronics NV, and Renault. The foundation was set up to promote the use of total quality management and best-management practices as a way of improving the global competitiveness and effectiveness of European businesses. The foundation launched the European Quality Award in 1991. This annual award is given to companies that best meet the EFQM criteria of management excellence.

The EFQM excellence model has evolved considerably since its conception by benchmarking against other organizational quality frameworks such as the Malcolm Baldrige National Quality Award in the United States, the South African and Australian Quality Award schemes, and the Japanese Deming Prize.

The EFQM excellence model is now widely recognized across Europe as an effective way of improving organizational performance. The model is applied and monitored through self-assessment and can be administered internally. Qualified external facilitators can also be called on to validate the self-assessment. The framework can be applied to any type or size of organization, at any stage of maturity, and to any size unit: the whole organization, a department, or a team. Tens of thousands of organizations, large and small, private sector, and not-for-profit across Europe, use the EFQM framework of good management practice for self-evaluation.

The EFQM Excellence Model

The basic framework of the EFQM excellence model, shown in Figure 14–1, consists of eight fundamental concepts:

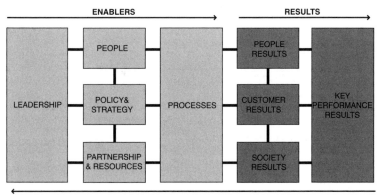

Figure 14–1   The European Foundation for Quality Management Excellence model

- Leadership and constancy of purpose
- People development and involvement
- Partnership development
- Management by processes and facts
- Customer focus including client collaboration and the measurement of customer satisfaction
- Society focus—corporate social responsibility and sustainable development
- Results orientation—key performance outcomes and indicators

The model incorporates a continuous learning feedback loop that promotes innovation and continuous improvement.

The basic principle of the EFQM excellence model is that there are many approaches to achieving sustainable excellence but that in general:

> Excellence Results with respect to Performance, Customers, People and Society are achieved through Leadership driving Policy and Strategy, People, Partnerships and Resources, and Processes. (EFQM)

The application of the EFQM excellence model (http://www.efqm.org/) consists of answering a series of questions that focus on each of the enablers, each of the results, and the continuous learning and innovation feedback loop shown in Figure 14–1. Scores for each component of the questionnaire are mapped against maturity models and can be benchmarked against profiles of companies in the same sector, including those that have won the European Quality Award.

Integrating EFQM and CTT

The Centre for Integral Excellence at Sheffield Hallam University is leading a consortium of universities in a study to evaluate the benefits of using the EFQM excellence model to improve organizational effectiveness in higher education in the United Kingdom. In the course of this work, the Centre has adopted the integral approach of Ken Wilber as a way of mapping the impacts of different methodologies on organizational excellence.

This approach led them to the understanding that the EFQM excellence model mainly looks at an organization from the perspective of the collective external quadrant—an objective view of an organization's collective behaviors. The seven levels of consciousness model, on the other hand, looks at the organization from the perspective of the internal individual and collective quadrants—a subjective internal view of the organization based on causal factors emanating from the individual and group consciousness. These perspectives are represented in Figure 14–2.

In the research undertaken thus far, the Centre for Integral Excellence has combined these two approaches to identify multiple areas of improvement for the higher education sector. They found that using

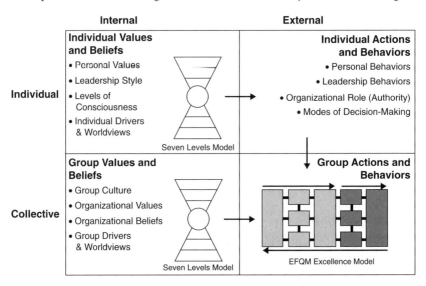

Figure 14–2   The European Foundation for Quality Management Excellence model and seven levels of consciousness model related to the integral model

this integrated methodologic approach with its different perspectives on organizational effectiveness yielded opportunities for the improvement of higher education in all four quadrants. The main improvements that have been found to be necessary, superimposed on the four quadrants of the integral model, are shown in Table 14–1.

As part of their research, the Centre for Integral Excellence has developed a maturity matrix for each of the nine criteria of the EFQM excellence model based on the seven levels of consciousness model. This seven-level, nine-characteristic evaluation matrix is shown in Figure 14–3. The vertical axis of this matrix provides a values-based dimension

Table 14–1   Improvements in Higher Education Allocated to the Integral Model

	Internal Values and Beliefs	External Actions and Behaviors
Individual	Leadership development Personal development	Performance appraisal Personal development plans Improved communication
Collective	Values alignment with staff Values alignment with students Values-driven culture	Continuous improvement Impact on local communities Improved collaboration with clients and staff Performance measurement through an integral or whole system scorecard including: — Values management — Risk management — Sustainability — Systems and processes

	Leadership	Policy & Strategy	People	Partnerships & Resources	Processes	Customer Results	People Results	Society Results	Key Performance Results
7	Wisdom/ Visionary Long-term sustainability	Strategic Plan for Sustain-ability	Opportunity to Serve Humanity	Develop Natural Resource Strategy	Natural Processes	Sustainability Ecology	Sustainability Ecology	Sustainability Ecology	Sustainability Index
6	Mentor/ Partner Cooperate with stakeholders	Dialogue With Stake-holders	Opportunity to Make a Difference Mentoring	Strategic Alliances	Value-Chain Development	Customer Collaboration	Employee Fulfillment	Community Relationships	Strategic Partnership Scorecard
5	Integrator/ Inspirer Create shared Vision/values	Build Cultural Resilience	Meaningful Work Creativity	Build Cooperation	process Integration	Values Assessment	Values Assessment	Values Assessment	Values Alignment Cultural Entropy
4	Facilitator/ Influencer Empowerment of employees	Continuous Learning	Personal Development	Continuous Improvement	Continuous Improvement & New Products/ Services	New Products & Services	Continuous Education & Development	Freedom of Choice	Balance Scorecard
3	Manager/ Organizer Implement best practice systems	Build Structural Resilience	Professional Development	Effective Resource Utilization	Productivity Efficiency Quality Standards	Volume of Sales	Employee Productivity	Energy and Resource Utilization	Productivity Efficiency Quality
2	Relationship Manager/ Communicator Develop stakeholder relationships	Communication with Stakeholders	Friendship & Collegiality	Conflict Resolution	Customer Relationshios	Customer Satisfaction	Employee Satisfaction	Stakeholder Satisfaction	Supplier Performance
1	Crisis Director/ Accountant Ensure financial stability	Financial Planning/ Open Book Management	Health & Safety	Building the Infrastructure	Financial Effectiveness	Value of Sales, Low Complaints & Returns	Low Absenteeism	Compliance to Environmental Standards	Profits Financial Stability
EFQM Evaluation Concepts	Leadership	Policy & Strategy	People	Partnerships & Resources	Processes	Customer Results	People Results	Society Results	Key Performance Results

ENABLERS: THE THINGS YOU DO (Activities, policies, strategies, approaches)	RESULTS: THE THINGS YOU MEASURE (Key Performance Indicators)

Figure 14–3   European Foundation for Quality Management Excellence model related to the seven levels of consciousness model

to mapping the maturity of the EFQM concepts. Further developments envisaged include the integration of a spiral dynamics perspective to the evaluation matrix.

A key learning from this work is the significance of the relationship between improving processes and a whole-system approach to cultural transformation. Higher education establishments operate as departmental silos with hierarchical command structures. Consequently, most improvements focus on reengineering of individual processes. There is no systemic or holistic approach to organization improvement and the values perspective is frequently ignored.

While the integral approach involving EFQM and CTT is still in its testing stages, the results of applying this matrix to higher education establishments is yielding deep insights into organizational performance.

Case Study: Facilities Directorate, Sheffield Hallam University

Sheffield Hallam is a complex organization of more than 3,000 employees and 28,000 students and has an annual budget of more than $300 million. The Facilities Directorate is a major business unit within this complex, with 560 employees and a budget of over $40 million. It provides a wide range of services including real estate management and maintenance, conference management, catering, cleaning, and hotel services.

In 1996 the Facilities Directorate succeeded in being the first business unit within the University to achieve the Investors in People (IiP) standard. The IiP standard is a "straightforward, proven framework for delivering business improvement through people." The achievement of this award is a demonstration of the directorate's commitment to the workforce through training and development, and effective communications. The IiP standard has since been re-awarded to the directorate with distinction.

For 6 years, the directorate has been using the EFQM excellence model as a tool for self-evaluation and business planning. As a result, it has implemented a wide range of policies and strategies that align with the EFQM concepts: leadership and people development, integrated planning, partnership development, and process management. It has also developed a comprehensive performance management system to track its progress in achieving its goals.

In July 2005, the directorate carried out a cultural values assessment using the CTT. The objective of this assessment was to explore the relationship between the seven levels of organizational consciousness and the nine criteria of the EFQM excellence model. The results of the values assessment are shown in Figure 14–4.

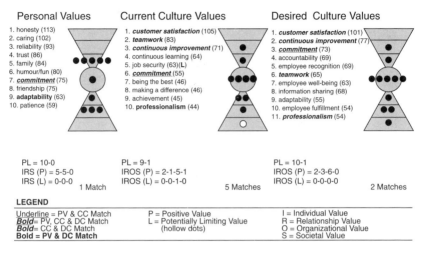

Figure 14–4 Values assessment for the Sheffield Hallam University
Facilities Directorate

It is important to note that except for the potentially limiting value of "job security,"[1] the directorate is close to operating from full-spectrum consciousness. However, the results of the cultural values assessment indicate that there are several issues that need to be resolved:

(1) The need for more focus on employee issues as denoted by the values of employee recognition, employee well-being, and employee fulfillment in the desired culture. The low number of matching personal and current culture values reinforces this

---

[1] Given the enormous changes that have take place at the university over the past few years and the general employment issues in the Sheffield area, people are not only happy to have a job, they are enthusiastic about their work. Consequently, there is very little evidence in the Facilities Directorate of the complacency and low productivity that usually accompany the value of job security. The strong showing of the value of "commitment" in the current culture supports this premise.

finding and begs the question, "To what extent are employees able to bring their full selves to work?"

(2) The need for greater efficiency and productivity as denoted by the values of accountability and information sharing in the desired culture.

(3) The need for more emphasis on relationships as denoted by the strong focus on relationship values in the employees' personal values (IRS [P] = 5 − 5 − 0) and the jump in the number of relationship values between the current (1) and the desired culture (3) in the IROS.

On the positive side, there is a strong acceptance, willingness, and readiness for continuous improvement and change as denoted by the strong emphasis given to level 4 consciousness in the current and desired cultures.

Based on the insights provided by the EFQM evaluation and CTT, a seven-level, nine-criteria maturity map has been developed for the Facilities Directorate (Figure 14–5). The shading codes on this diagram are the same as those used in Chapter 11. White corresponds to strong performance; black corresponds to weak performance.

There are significant similarities between the areas for improvement identified by the EFQM assessment and CTT assessment—employee issues: employee commitment, employee recognition; and employee fulfillment and performance issues regarding information sharing and accountability (empowerment). Through the lens of the seven-level, nine-criteria matrix, we see that the most significant arenas for improvement are leadership—particularly with regard to the development of emotional intelligence skills (manager/employee relationships) and the management of external stakeholder relationships. The third arena for improvement is the field of processes and process integration. The cultural values assessment shows that the current level of cultural entropy

	Leadership	Policy & Strategy	People	Partnerships & Resources	Processes	Customer Results	People Results	Society Results	Key Performance Results
7	Wisdom/ visionary Long-term Sustainaviliy	Strategic Plan for Sustainability	Opportunity to Serve Humanity	Develop Natural Resource Strategy	Natural Processes	Sustainability Ecology	Sustainability Ecology	Sustainability Ecology	Sustainability Index
6	Mentor/ Partner Cooperate with stakeholders	Dialogue With Stake-holders	Opportunity to Make a Difference Mentoring	Strategic Alliances	Values-Chain Development	Customer Collaboration	Employee Fulfillment	Community Relationships	Strategic Partnership Scorecard
5	Integrator/ Inspirer Create shared vision/values	Build Cultural Resilience	Meaningful Work Creativity	Build Cooperation	Process Integration	Values Assessment	Values Assessment	Values Assessment	Values Alignment Cultural Entropy
4	Facilitator/ Influencer Empower employees	Continuous Learning	Personal Development	Continuous Improvement	Continuous Improvement & New Products/ Services	New Products & Services	Continuous Education & Personal Development	Freedom of Choice	Balance Scorecard
3	Manager/ Organizer Implement best-practice systems	Build Structural Resilience	Professional Development	Effective Resource Utilization	Productivity, Efficiency, Quality Standards	Volume of Sales	Employee Productivity	Energy and Resource Utilization	Productivity Efficiency Quality
2	Relationship Manager/ Communicator Develop stakeholder relationships	Communication with Stakeholders	Friendship & Collegiality Communication strategy	Conflict Resolution	Customer Relationships	Customer Satisfaction	Employee Satisfaction	Stakeholder Satisfaction	Supplier Performance
1	Crisis Director/ Accountant Ensure financial stability	Financial Planning/ Open Book Management	Health & Safety	Building the Infrastructure	Financial Effectiveness	Value of Sales, Low Complaints & Returns	Low Absenteeism	Compliance to Environmental Standards	Profits Financial Stability
EFQM Evaluation Concepts	Leadership	Policy & Strategy	People	Partnerships & Resources	Processes	Customer Results	People Results	Society Results	Key Performance Results
	ENABLERS: THE THINGS YOU DO (Activities, policies, strategies, approaches)					RESULTS: THE THINGS YOU MEASURE (Key Performance Indicators)			

Figure 14–5   European Foundation for Quality Management Excellence/seven levels of consciousness maturity matrix for the Sheffield Hallam University Facilities Directorate

is 18%, indicating the need for some cultural adjustment improvements, but no significant or serious issues.

The most prevalent potentially limiting values in the current culture are information hoarding, bureaucracy, and hierarchy. These values tend to denote leadership issues with regard to cooperation, empowerment, and trust—issues that relate to employee fulfillment and the seamless integration of people's activities across institutional boundaries and levels. The Directorate's future challenges are to give more emphasis to employee empowerment and recognition, build stronger stakeholder relationships, and break down the institutional barriers that are preventing cooperation and coordination.

Over the past 6 years the EFQM excellence model has undoubtedly provided the Facilities Directorate with a robust framework of quantifiable and qualitative management information that has led to significant improvements in performance and has contributed to the directorate being recognized as a leader in its field. The management dashboard is much more "balanced" than it was before the adoption of the EFQM model. The addition of the CTT assessment to the EFQM evaluation process provides an additional "values-management" or cultural spectrum to the directorate's management dashboard that was previously missing. It is causing the directorate to reflect on and give more emphasis to leadership values and behaviors (culture). This added dimension will be a key factor in developing the directorate's people, partnership, and stakeholder strategies as it continues its journey toward integral excellence and full-spectrum consciousness.

15

New Leaders,
New Change Agents

In conclusion, I would like to draw the reader's attention to what I believe is the key concept of this book.

Values-Based Decision Making

For the most part, the decisions we make each day as individuals and groups are based on our subconscious and conscious beliefs about satisfying our individual and collective needs. These beliefs are a reflection of our personal and cultural conditioning concerning what we have to do to maintain or enhance our individual or collective internal stability and external equilibrium within the framework of our existence.

As we evolve and grow as individuals and groups, we adapt our worldviews so that we are able to maintain internal stability and external equilibrium in increasingly complex situations. As long as those situations are defined by a shared culture where we are dealing with people who, like ourselves, operate from similar beliefs because they experienced the same enculturation process, beliefs are adequate for making decisions that help us maintain or enhance our internal stability and external equilibrium.

However, when we are called to make decisions in a larger or a global framework of existence where we encounter people who have experienced a different enculturation process and do not share our beliefs, then beliefs no longer form a valid framework for collective decision making. In such situations, our beliefs separate us from each other. The only mind space where we can meet people who operate from different beliefs is the mind space defined by our most deeply held values—the values that are part of our collective soul experience. Soul-based values are universal. They unite us rather than separate us. Beliefs are always contextual, whereas values are concepts that transcend all contexts. They are common to the whole of humanity.

To move into the mind space of values-based decision making we must be willing to let go of some of our beliefs—more specifically, we must let go of the subconscious and conscious *fear-based* beliefs that influence our day-to-day decision making. These are the beliefs that separate us from each other. This process is called *self-actualization*. In this process, the "self" that is actualized represents the soul-self: the self that is able to transcend the conditioning of the enculturation process; the self that frees us from the beliefs of the past that we accepted without thinking because we wanted to belong, and we wanted to be respected by our peers; the self that is a composite blend of the positive beliefs held by the ego and the values held by the soul.

The reason self-actualization leads to freedom is because it loosens the bonds of enculturation. We become free to choose our own path, our own way of being—a way of being that may be different from our parents and our peers. We can only do this in a democracy or a governance structure that respects individual differences; a structure that accepts and is comfortable with diversity; a structure where everyone has a voice and where different beliefs are celebrated as long as they do not undermine the internal stability of the whole.

Self-actualization occurs when we are able to let go, tame, or manage the subconscious fear-based beliefs that are held by the ego. For self-actualization to occur, we must align the accumulation of positive beliefs held by the ego with the universal values held by the soul. As we progress down this path and we activate soul consciousness, we automatically shift from belief-based decision making to values-based decision making. At the same time, the ego-based drivers that are represented by the red, blue, orange, and green worldviews give way to the soul-based drivers represent by the yellow and turquoise worldviews.

The self that is operating in the self-actualized mind space is a self that has mastered the satisfaction of the belief-based needs of not having enough (survival consciousness), not being loved (relationship consciousness), and not being enough (self-esteem consciousness). It is a self that is concerned about the greater good because it has freed itself from its personal fears. It is a self that cannot live with inequality. It wants everyone to have similar opportunities.

During the process of self-actualization our minds change. The ego-based drivers that dominate the lower levels of consciousness evolve into the soul-based drivers that dominate the upper levels of consciousness. Instead of focusing on our ego-based personal survival, relationship, and self-esteem needs, we focus on our personal soul-based needs—finding meaning in existence, actualizing that meaning by making a difference in our world, and finally when making a difference becomes a way of life, entering into the realm of self-less service.

Full-Spectrum Leaders

The preceding concepts have major implications for our future leaders. In an increasingly complex interconnected world, where uncertainty dominates, we need leaders who have transcended the fear-based beliefs that formed part of their personal and collective enculturation. We need leaders who are fearless and who operate on behalf of the global common good. We need self-actualized leaders who predominantly operate with yellow and turquoise worldviews and who use values as their predominant mode of decision making. We need leaders who embrace diversity, celebrate differences, and give people a voice. Above all else, we need leaders we can trust; leaders who we know have our best interests at heart; leaders who recognize our individual contributions; and leaders who encourage and support their people in their professional and personal growth. We need leaders that operate from full-spectrum consciousness.

Master Practitioners of Whole-System Change

These concepts also have major implications for our future change agents—the people who support our leaders in bringing about whole-system change. They must be self-actualized individuals who predominantly operate with yellow and turquoise worldviews. In addition, they must be master practitioners of whole-system change. They must be versed in the seven levels of consciousness, the eight worldviews, appreciative inquiry, and numerous other methodologies and techniques that are used in designing a whole-system change process that will increase the cultural, operational, and functional resilience of the organization or community in which they are working. Everything they do must be based on an integral understanding of the world in which they operate. If they are operating in the business arena, they must also be versed in business. If they are operating in the community arena, they must also be versed in politics. Finally, they must understand the importance of working in the causal realms of the individual and the collective by supporting leaders and leadership teams in their individual and collective transformation. They must know how to set up and customize values-management systems to monitor the process of change and the achievement of the targets and goals the leader, the leadership group and the people want to see.

To these ends, I have committed the rest of my life to the following:

(1) Building a global cadre of master practitioners of whole-system change that can support self-actualized leaders in creating a values-driven future for business, for civil society, and for humanity as a whole, and

(2) Providing leadership training programs that build self-actualized, full-spectrum business and political leaders who can create the values-based world that our souls are yearning to see.

For those of you who are leaders, your challenge is to recognize that the impact you have on the world depends on your ability to grow in consciousness—to become a full-spectrum leader. You will need to seek out master practitioners of whole-system change who can support you in your endeavors.

For those of you who are practitioners, your challenge is not only to grow in consciousness but also to equip yourselves with an understanding of the models and tools that allow you to design and customize integral approaches to whole-system change to support the leaders you work with in creating a positive future for their organizations and the communities that they serve.

Appendix

Resources and Contact Information

Appreciative Inquiry

Sallie Lee
Shared Sun Studio
E-mail: Sallie@sharedsun.net
Website: www.sharedsun.net

Balanced Scorecard

Sally Mizerak
E-mail: Sallymizerak@performancedrivers.net
Website: www.performancedrivers.net

Baldrige National Quality Program

Website: www.quality.nist.gov/

Centre for Integral Studies, Sheffield Hallam University

Mike Pupius
E-mail: m.pupius@shu.ac.uk
Website: www.shu.ac.uk/integralexcellence

Coaching

Tom Brady
E-mail: tbrady@thexlr8team.com
Website: www.thexlr8team.com

Cultural Transformation Tools (CTT)

Richard Barrett
Richard Barrett & Associates
E-mail: Richard@valuescentre.com
Website: www.valuescentre.com

European Foundation for Quality Management (EFQM)

Website: www.efqm.org

Mentoring

David Carter
Merryck & Co.
E-mail: david.carter@merryck.com
Website: www.merryck.com

Resilience

Steve Trevino
Resilience Matrix
E-mail: global_sustainability@netzero.net
Website: resiliencematrix.com

Spiral Dynamics

Dr. Don Beck
E-mail: drbeck@attglobal.net
Website: www.spiraldynamics.net

Theater

Erik Muten
E-mail: erik@dramaworks.com
Website: www.dramaworks.com

Values-Based Leadership: Business Simulation

Ed Manning
Richard Barrett & Associates
E-mail: Ed@valuescentre.com
Website: www.valuescentre.com/leaders/vbl.htm

Values-Management Software

Richard Barrett
Richard Barrett & Associates
E-mail: Richard@valuescentre.com
Website: www.valuescentre.com
and
Morel Fourman
Gaiasoft International
E-mail: solutions@gaiasoft.com
Website: www.gaiasoft.com

Index

227